I have been privileged to know five ᶃ family. She writes with a legacy of l is both precious and powerful. Her perspective from pulpit to back row pew, from childhood to spiritual mother to many, from hurts to healing is endearing, edifying, and moving. You will love Christ and His bride more by reading these inspiring insights generated by generations of faithfulness.

BRYAN CHAPELL
Presbyterian Church in America Stated Clerk, Lawrenceville, Georgia

One thing I know for certain about Katie Polski is that she loves the Church and I can think of no one better suited to write *Beyond the Back Row* than her. This book is an invitation for believers to love Christ's Church as He loves her. Katie enjoins readers to not forsake gathering in worship, to serve the local Body, and to engage in community with other believers. *Beyond the Back Row* is highly practical and deeply biblical as it encourages believers to love the Bride that Christ died to save.

CHRISTINA FOX
Author, *Closer than a Sister: How Union with Christ Helps Friendships to Flourish*

Katie Polski's unique view from the pew as both a Pastor's Kid and now a Pastor's wife cultivates a high view of Christ's Bride. Consider this book a primer on forsaking a consumeristic approach to the Church and embracing the Covenant beauty and blessing of belonging to God's family of families.

KAREN HODGE
Coordinator, Presbyterian Church in America Women's Ministries; Author, *Transformed: Life-taker to Life-giver*

Beyond the Back Row

Rediscovering the Beauty of the Local Church for Your Family

Katie Polski

CHRISTIAN
FOCUS

Copyright © Katie Polski 2025

paperback ISBN 978-1-5271-1265-0
ebook ISBN 978-1-5271-1312-1

10 9 8 7 6 5 4 3 2 1

Published in 2025
by
Christian Focus Publications Ltd,
Geanies House, Fearn, Ross-shire,
IV20 1TW, Great Britain.

www.christianfocus.com

Cover design by
Daniel van Straaten

Printed and bound by
Bell & Bain, Glasgow

In memory of my mom and dad who taught me by example what it means to love Christ's bride.

—

To Ella, Cooper, Jonathan, and Lily: To cultivate a love for the church in the next generation is to plant seeds of faith that we pray will grow into a legacy of service and unwavering commitment to Christ. I pray, by God's grace, you will continue planting those seeds for the next generation.

—

To Chris: In the journey of faith and service to the church, you have been my steadfast companion. May the Lord see fit to give us many more years serving God's church together.

Table of Contents

Introduction

I grew up as a "PK." This does *not* stand for "Potential Kid" which was the best guess of a friend in elementary school. I was a pastor's kid, and this status resulted in some interesting conversations through the years. When I was young, I asked a friend if she wanted to come over and play after church, and her response left an imprint: "Well, I want to, but how long do you guys actually pray before lunch? Like an hour?" It was an honest question. A child's fear of leaving church only to have to go home and pray for an hour before consuming food was a legitimate concern.

I remember considering my answer. *How long do we actually pray? Is it an hour?* I didn't think it was, though some prayers over meals certainly felt longer than others, but to secure the play date, I told her we did super quick prayers. So, she agreed to come over for the afternoon. As we walked out to the car, I remember asking God to help my dad keep his lunch prayer super quick.

Along with having dad as our pastor, our mom was the children's choir director, so we sat under her tutelage in the church as well. I remember my first Sunday night in her kid's choir rehearsal because I had a significant revelation: my mom put actual time and effort into her choir preparations. I just figured she showed up, told the kids to sing, and they sang. This was not exactly the case. It turns out that kids need structure, which takes planning, and kids also need incentives, which my mom took care of with candy. There was ample candy, and so we sang. Mom would unabashedly wave her arms producing more volume and more energy from her choirs, and when we sang out to her liking, the candy followed. I loved children's choir.

As a child, I was often asked, *"What is it like to have a dad as a pastor?"* I thought it was great. Despite the peculiar conversations related to being a "PK," my two sisters and I had fun with all the "perks" that came with having a dad as a pastor, including free reign of the church building. We spent a lot of time in our church, which was across the street from our childhood home. Only a quaint bridge separated the two properties. Church was such a welcoming place that we even asked dad if we could go with him on Saturdays when he walked over to work on his Sunday sermon. He'd usually agree, and then give us access to most of the church building, a dream for mischievous kids with vivid imaginations.

The three of us were like little church mice while growing up, scampering from room to room; we were there when the doors opened and there when they closed. We were as comfortable in the building as we were in our own home, and for many years, my sisters and I watched as our parents labored faithfully and joyfully within its walls. Over time, my love for the church transformed from a liking of the actual church building, and all the space that allowed my imagination to soar, to a genuine love for the elements of worship and the people of God, and my parents' view of the local church played a huge part in my growing affection for the body of Christ. They regarded church ministry enthusiastically: they loved the people, they loved the various ministries, and they loved worship. Their passion for the local church was infectious, and even at a young age, I caught it. My appreciation for the church has continued to grow in deep and unique ways through the years, and I'm grateful to the Lord for that.

I'm also very aware that my experience is not necessarily common; in fact, it is an increasingly unusual experience. Along with being a pastor's wife, I currently work as the music director at our church, and one Sunday I had off from leading, so I decided to sit in the back row to gain a different perspective. It had been a while since I'd sat toward the back, and as I took in the experience from this viewpoint, I had the thought: *church is strange.* If I was new, observing the rituals and beliefs that step out of societal norms, I would wonder about this place and question its sometimes perplexing doctrines and practices. I suddenly realized I didn't know the people sitting on my right and left and was acutely grateful that my back seat was near the exit. I thought about how many people, without a proper understanding of the beauty, necessity, and purpose of the church, dwell on its peculiarity and in turn wonder, *why commit?*

It's a legitimate question. As much as this book is for those former church mice, like me, who need a refreshed perspective on why to stay invested in the local church, this book is also for the "back rowers" who wonder what the point of church really is, or who have been hurt by it in the past and so come skeptically and reservedly. I've had many conversations with churchgoers from all differing perspectives throughout this writing process, and while the varying levels of involvement in, and love for, the church runs the gamut, the pendulum seems to be increasingly swinging toward the side of distrust and skepticism of the local church.

When I was a child, family involvement in a church was somewhat typical amongst neighbors, but over the years, church attendance has dropped drastically, even amongst Bible-believing Christians. According to various surveys, both church frequency and overall church attendance among Christians is on the decline. Twenty years ago, roughly 42 per cent of U.S. adults attended religious services every week, but now this figure is down to just about 30 per cent.[1] Many pastors

---

and other church leaders predict the downward trend of church attendance will continue, perhaps even more drastically in the next generation. This is not a book that explores *why* this is the case; rather, my attempt is to encourage people of all ages, and in all different stages of life, to *reconsider the importance of the local church in their own lives and in the lives of the next generation so that we might have a deep and abiding faith in Jesus.* The purpose of our involvement is not really about the institution of the church in and of itself, but it's about Christ, and our faith in Him. Our commitment to His church, His bride, is one of the greatest ways we can grow in our relationship with Jesus.

When we talk about the commitment to the church in the next generation, ensuring that children remain devoted to a local church body is not a simple math equation. Parents can't do a little of "this" and add a little of "that" and simply produce active, God-fearing church members. Not at all. In fact, the Bible makes clear that this kind of result is the work of the Holy Spirit in an individual's heart. Jesus alone saves our children and draws them to Him, and their stories are written by Jesus, not by us.

But we do have a responsibility as parents, spiritual-parents, and believers in Christ to consider how we view the significance of the church in our own lives and how we can cultivate a love for the church in the next generation. The Lord has worked on my heart in distinct ways to enrich my understanding of the importance of His church, but I have no doubt that even in their imperfection, the Lord used my parent's example to plant a desire to embrace, love, and serve the body of Christ.

Each person has a different story when it comes to their background with the church. Some have been significantly hurt by it, and so have kept this community at bay; others

---

services/#:~:text=According%20to%20Gallup's%20data%2C%20this,figure%20is%20just%2030%20percent.

have struggled to find the right "fit" for their family, spending years hopping from one church to the next, and there are some who used to be committed to a church but have lost sight of its significance because they've become jaded by difficult members or unending hypocrisy. And many families today have simply embraced the convenience of online worship, making the return to their local church less essential, at least in their own eyes.

No matter what your experience, whether you are a faithful attender or an infrequent backseat warmer, the Bible makes the importance of the local church utterly clear, and if it has significant value to Jesus, *it must hold a place of significance in our own lives.* Ask the Lord to refocus your vision to see His church the way He does. Doing so will help us better understand how to embrace and love the bride of Christ. The local church is one of the most profound communities a person can be a part of and, because of this, we should actively pursue ways we can better love and appreciate the church in our own lives and understand how we can better teach its beauty and significance to the next generation.

PART ONE:
Why the Church?

…That you, being rooted and grounded in love, may have strength to comprehend with all the saints what is the breadth and length and height and depth, and to know the love of Christ that surpasses knowledge, that you may be filled with all the fullness of God. Now to him who is able to do far more abundantly than all that we ask or think, according to the power at work within us, to him be glory in the church and in Christ Jesus throughout all generations, forever and ever. Amen.

Ephesians 3:17b-21

1

The Purpose of the Local Church

I know a couple who picked a Bible verse when they were married that they felt represented a vision for their newly-formed family. Many years later, the father died unexpectedly, leaving behind a widow and three adult children. At his funeral, I was struck by how much their family's verse surfaced as a central theme. And then, when our Bible study group came across the verse one week, I listened as the dear widow became emotional and shared the significance of these words, not just for her but for her children and grandchildren. I know this family well, and each individual member is so different from each other in personality and giftedness, and yet, they are united under one single, biblical purpose.

For many reasons, this is a beautiful image of the local church. In one sense there is only one church: "There is one body and one Spirit – just as you were called to the one hope that belongs to your call – one Lord, one faith, one baptism, one God and Father of all, who is over all and through all and in all (Eph. 4:4-6). There is **one** body and **one** Spirit, which means that as children of God we are one family, unified in Christ. This verse reminds us that in Jesus, our commonality is far greater than any of our differences. Each believer in Jesus represents this Universal church, and there will be a day when we will all worship together in eternity as one, singing praises to our God and Father, Jesus Christ. The diversity will be seen, and the commonality of our faith evident above all: every tribe, every tongue, and every language will be represented, all uniting as one body under Christ (Rev. 7:9-10). What a day that will be!

There is a single Greek word that we translate as "church" in the New Testament, and it is *ekklesia.* This word is made up of two Greek words: *ek,* which means "out from and to," and *kaleo,* which means "to call." Seeing this translation, the word literally means, "the called-out ones." The universal church is called to Jesus and called out to the work of His Kingdom.

While we are a part of the larger family of God, we have been given the gift of the local church which we find established in the New Testament. Many of Paul's letters are written to encourage and exhort individual churches toward this goal, and it's significant to note that each church he writes to has unique challenges and responsibilities within their time and place. But even within the differing make-up of personalities and callings, we can still find common, biblical goals for all "called out ones" who are a part of the local church.

The Local Church Exists to Bring Glory to God

The local church is not just about the people in it; in fact, it's not even about the pastors or elders who are called to lead. The church is about Jesus. In Ephesians 3, Paul offers a prayer of spiritual strength for the body of believers in Ephesus. Verses 17-21 are some of my favorite verses, and they pointedly remind believers about the power and purpose of church: "...That you, being rooted and grounded in love, may have strength to comprehend with all the saints what is the breadth and length and height and depth, and to know the love of Christ that surpasses knowledge, that you may be filled with all the fullness of God. Now to him who is able to do far more abundantly than all that we ask or think, according to the power at work within us, to him be glory in the church and in Christ Jesus throughout all generations, forever and ever. Amen."

Prior to these verses, Paul prays that the church in Ephesus would know the never-ending love of God. What follows naturally is the reminder that they can *really know* this love in and through the strength of Christ who is able to do for us far beyond what we can imagine. Just relish these words for a moment. Consider the greatest experience you have ever had. God is able to provide exceedingly far more. Now imagine the greatest scenario that could ever be. God is able to do more than that. Charles Spurgeon points out that the phrase "far more abundantly" is really a Greek expression made up by Paul. In other words, the apostle could not find language superlative enough to describe God's abilities, and so he simply made up a phrase that in his mind best encapsulated the goodness of God. This is the amazing God we serve, and He deserves glory in all things, including work done in the local church. And, in God's perfect providence, His love and goodness is *experienced* within the church. John Stott says of these verses:

> We shall have power to comprehend these dimensions of Christ's love...only with all the saints. The isolated Christian can indeed know something of the love of Jesus. But his grasp is bound to be limited by his limited experience. It needs the whole people of God to understand the whole love of God, all the saints together, Jews and Gentiles, men and women, young and old, black and white, with all their varied backgrounds and experiences.[2]

What a magnificent picture. We need each other, and through each other, we bring praise to our God who is able, that He may be glorified and that others may know of His great love. This applies to making the coffee on a Sunday morning as much as it does to those leading in worship. You bring glory to God as you serve the littlest in the congregation by loving on them in the

---

2.   John Stott, *God's New Society: The Message of Ephesians.* (InterVarsity, 1979), p. 137.

nursery or teaching them during Sunday School, and you bring God glory when you fulfill the call to love the widows in your congregation (James 1:27). You can even bring glory to God when cleaning up the bathrooms or the kitchen or resetting the chairs.

Every deed of ministry in the local church can proclaim Christ, and if that is our focus, if that is our goal, then we are glorifying our Creator in great ways as we serve His church. 2 Corinthians 4:5 reminds us that "what we proclaim is not ourselves, but Jesus Christ as Lord, with ourselves as your servants for Jesus' sake." We come together in these groups of believers each with different backgrounds, varying baggage, and unique personalities all to proclaim Christ and give glory to God. The same power that raised Jesus from the dead is the power at work in each person who claims Jesus as their Lord. Imagine how great that power is when we come together and collectively work and serve to the glory of God.

The Local Church Exists to Show God's Love to Others

Hebrews 10:24-25 says, "And let us consider how to stir up one another to love and good works, not neglecting to meet together, as is the habit of some, but encouraging one another, and all the more as you see the Day drawing near." As we meet in local communities, one of the purposes is to offer the love of God to our brother and sister in Christ, encouraging one another, and stirring up one another to love and to do good work. This idea of stirring up suggests that there is work involved in the process. I think about the plastic pool my dad would set up in the backyard when we were little. It was just big enough that we could stand, and the water would come up to our waist. One of our favorite things was to create a kind of whirlpool in the water by circling around the pool in the same direction, over and over, and as we picked up speed, the water would start carrying us along. This is the image of stirring up. It takes energy and initiative, but when used positively, the energy picks up and the love for one another begins to carry a body along.

And to do this, in order to show tangible love to one another, we must be meeting together on a regular basis. The church is meant for you to be blessed and to be a blessing, and these loving relationships extend to every age and every place in life, to every crisis, and every joy. All of it can be touched by the church community who stand as an extension of the hands and feet of Christ. There are other communities who often show genuine love and care; you may find support in your work or school communities, and if you do, be grateful for such a gift. But the church stands unique in its love and service to one another as a *God-ordained institution*, one where the means of grace flow from Him through the church members. This happens when we make public vows to be held accountable, as we partake in the sacraments, and as we worship and serve shoulder to shoulder with our brothers and sisters in Christ for a transcendent purpose. Our passions for Christian living are *stirred* as we live amongst other believers in our local church communities.

The Local Church Exists to Spread God's Love Throughout the World

The Great Commission found in Matthew 28:18-20 cannot be overlooked when talking about the purpose of the local church:

> And Jesus came and said to them, "All authority in heaven and on earth has been given to me. Go therefore and make disciples of all nations, baptizing them in the name of the Father and of the Son and of the Holy Spirit, teaching them to observe all that I have commanded you. And behold, I am with you always, to the end of the age.

While we are cared for, challenged, and stretched within the walls of the building, the body of believers must always have an outward gaze. We grow spiritually in our local churches, experiencing God's transformation of our hearts, not simply to keep the good news of the gospel to ourselves, but to go out and make disciples. We grow in our love for one another, stirring each other up so that we have the strength to teach others about God's commands, and we do all this knowing that God has promised that He will be with us always, "even to the end of the age."

One of my favorite hymns is *The Church's One Foundation*, and every time I sing verse four, my eyes swell and my heart soars:

> *The Church shall never perish!*
> *Her dear Lord to defend,*
> *to guide, sustain, and cherish*
> *is with her to the end.*
> *Tho' there be those that hate her,*
> *and strive to see her fail,*
> *against both foe and traitor*
> *she ever shall prevail.*

With the Lord to defend, guide, sustain, and cherish, the church *will* prevail, just as is promised in 1 Peter 1:23: "Since you have been born again, not of perishable seed but of imperishable, through the living and abiding word of God." We are born again through the Word of God, and it is His Word that will sustain the church. How can we *not* be excited to share the grace of Jesus found in His abiding Word with those who have not yet understood it? With all that has, and will, fail us in this life, to be able to tell someone about the gospel of Jesus which will *never* perish is a gift we cannot keep to ourselves.

There's no doubt that, at times, it's difficult to invite others into a church to hear the Word of God. Maybe we don't see the church as inviting, or perhaps instead of seeing the church as a beautiful body of believers, we tend to focus on some of the ugliness that exists within its walls. Each church is made up of sinners, broken and in need of Jesus, and we need to be honest about this reality, which is why our message to the unbelieving world is not to come and experience a community of humans who have it all figured out, but to come and witness a grace-filled community that embraces the graciousness of our great God.

For those who have trouble seeing the church in this light, it may be the fault of the leadership who've lost sight of gospel centrality or who have taken their eyes off the One who is their head. But for others, the beauty of the church and the grandeur of its purpose have simply never been experienced. These are people who might attend church occasionally, but who still don't see why it is worth investing in, who still aren't sure that what is being taught is really for them. The ones who feel this way are not the ones "out there," but they stand shoulder to shoulder with you in the pews on a Sunday morning. The call to be missional is as much to share the love of God with those who have never entered a church as it is to pay attention to those who you only see sporadically. If we stop caring about spreading the love of Jesus and only focus on what the church offers *me,* we can become jaded very quickly, or even worse, fall into apathy because this is not what God intended for His church. He calls us to make disciples, knowing that He is with us in every conversation, in every invite to a service, and even in the times we are belittled because of our faith. For those who claim Jesus as their Father, we must remember the purpose of God's church and pray that as we devote ourselves to its goals, God will work in and through us as vessels of His grace.

2

The Significance of the Local Church

We went to a running banquet for my son's cross-country team several years back. I knew the team was large, so I was prepared for a long a evening. I estimated the event might take two hours or so, but after four and a half hours, they were not even close to wrapping up. We finally called it a night and snuck out early, and I was astonished that more were not filing out early. Don't get me wrong, I was grateful for the time and care that went into individual speeches about each runner, but *four and half hours* of it was about good for me. As we drove home, my husband made a comment that I have not forgotten: "Well," he said, feeling a little guilt about our early departure, "people have to find their community somewhere."

His statement is so true. We were made for community; from the beginning of time this was the case when God made Eve so that Adam would not have to be alone. Our heavenly Father created us as people who thrive by living alongside one another. While I heard a few positive stories that came out of the lockdown during the COVID pandemic, it's clear that depression skyrocketed. There are many reasons for this, but one is simply that so many were living in isolation. This is not the way that God intended for us to live. And for church-goers, the isolation had a negative affect because we were out of sync with meeting and fellowship and worshipping and living amongst our brothers and sisters in our church communities.

Admittedly, there are times when I look around the sanctuary and think how odd it is, this group of people with whom I congregate week in and week out. These are not people whom I would necessarily otherwise know or socialize with. But I do know them. And our paths have not just crossed, but they are intertwined. And while it might seem strange at times, the people you look around and see on a Sunday morning matter in your life. The church matters. For every single believer in Christ, *the church matters.* This idea has been lost in our modern world because families tend to find their communities in different, more convenient places, like a cross-country team. If sports take priority, then it's natural that our teammates' families will become our community. If work takes priority, then our fellow employees become our source of fellowship. If pleasure is our goal, then our community might become the country club.

And what's the problem with this? That was a question posed when I gently pushed back in a conversation with someone who admitted that while they occasionally attend church, their children's school had really become their most significant community. The problem is that the church *should* take precedence over other spheres of influence in our life because the church is ordained by God to be used as the vessel through which He brings His kingdom to earth. No other institution can claim this!

The church is significant because it is an institution ordained by God, but it is also the only place where our involvement is imperative to our spiritual well-being. Through our local churches, we are offered the ability to be strengthened through the sacraments, hear teaching from God's Word, receive the accountability and encouragement necessary to stand firm in life's trials, and engage in worship that draws us closer to our Savior. If our communities are centered elsewhere, we lose out on the spiritual growth that occurs through God's church.

And most other places of community are not intended to last for a lifetime. One of the most common groups that replace involvement in the church is our children's school, but we lose the connectedness in these communities when our children graduate. Throughout our ministry, we've seen many couples struggle as empty nesters for this very reason. When we center our community around institutions that don't involve enduring covenantal relationships (relationships involving vows before God), we miss the significance of lifelong commitments that strengthen our horizontal relationships with each other and reflect our vertical relationship with Jesus. The reality is, those to whom you make promises in this life are the relationships that will be the strongest and last the longest. And if our activities are predominantly centered around communities that do not deal in the means of grace such as the Lord's Supper, the preaching of the Word, and prayer, then our spiritual well will quickly dry up because we are not regularly being reminded of the blood that was shed on our behalf, and the promise that, for all of eternity, God is our God and we are His people.

If our spiritual nourishment consistently comes from outside of the church, we miss out on the importance of accountability, doctrinally and relationally. Is it countercultural to invest in a church community? Yes. It absolutely is. But there is not another group that holds the kind of significance that the church does. In Matthew 16:18, Jesus tells Peter that "on this rock, I will build my church, and the gates of hell shall not prevail against it." Peter knows he is not the single rock on which Jesus will build His church, but he says that Jesus Himself is the cornerstone, and we, all of us as believers in Jesus, are the living stones that make up the church (1 Pet. 2:4-5). And with Jesus as the cornerstone, not even the greatest darkness imaginable, as Peter describes the gates of hell, can overcome the church of Jesus Christ. Jesus stands to defend His bride in any kind of tribulation or turmoil, amid persecution and hatred, He will defend His church against the very gates of hell. This is how much He loves His bride; we cannot love Jesus and not love His church. *This,* brothers and sisters, gives the church a uniquely transcendent significance.

3

Prioritizing the Local Church

We've heard far too many stories of parents with tweens and teens who have decided to put church involvement on the back burner. *"Just for now,"* many of them assure, and they explain that it's too much with sports and other social commitments to really invest in a local church community. Listen, I get the mayhem of life. I really do. But it's during this exact season that feels like we're barely keeping our heads above water that the church needs to be central in our family's life. There are few Christian parents who do not desire for their children to have a personal relationship with God and find a church home that fosters that relationship. If this is our desire for the next generation, then we need to set the pattern of centralizing church involvement while our children are still in the home.

Ultimately, the reason for prioritizing the church comes from the rule and reign of Christ. Without Jesus, the church is merely an entity like any other institution. It is true that the church itself can become an idol, and many need to be aware and be careful to not make the church more important than Christ. In Luke 10:27, Jesus exhorts us to "love the Lord your God with all your heart and with all your soul and with all your strength and with all your mind, and your neighbor as yourself." An idol is anything that we replace this love with. *Anything,* including the church. If you wonder if the church has become an idol, ask yourself: 1) Am I more enamored by my church's programs than I am my study of His word? 2) Am I more drawn to worship because the service gives me a good feeling or because it causes me to lift my eyes to Jesus? 3) Am I quickly willing to say how much I love my church, but I am more hesitant in mixed company to tell them how much I love my Savior? 4) Is my only time of spiritual connection when I'm at church?

Understanding His supremacy certainly keeps our view of the church in check. And, while the church should not be prioritized *over* our relationship with Christ, it must remain central in our weekly activities because *of the supremacy of our relationship with Christ.* This matters not just for us as individuals or as a family unit, but it matters for the church body as a whole. Your presence, your service, and your involvement make a difference in your church community. Not one person is insignificant in the body of believers. If we all began believing that lie, local churches would diminish very quickly, but prioritizing our engagement in the ministries of the church encourages, strengthens, and enhances the whole church body.

The New Testament Epistles were written to groups of believers who dedicated themselves to each other and to the gospel of Jesus. Because of this, many of the commands that are stated in these letters are written to consider in a corporate sense. If the church is merely something we attend when we have time, we cannot follow through in our communal commitment to do things like forgive each other (Eph. 4:32) and bear one another's burdens (Gal. 6:2). These and the other commands given throughout the Epistles are felt, learned, and applied when the church body takes precedence. In short, your presence matters to your local church! When the priority of church involvement is lost in the frenzy of everyday living, it not only affects you, but it affects others in the church community.

This is part of the reason why online church attendance should never become a permanent replacement for in-person worship. If we become satisfied with merely watching church online for a couple of hours on a Sunday morning, we're losing the centrality of the church in our family's lives. When we physically attend worship, we instinctively use all five senses, something that doesn't occur when we're watching online, and when our senses are aroused, our hearts naturally open to the beauty and importance of our surroundings.

When we were in quarantine in 2020, some friends made us the most delicious loaf of sourdough bread. I can show you a picture of it, and I can even describe the taste with vivid detail, but none of this compares to being in my kitchen, smelling and tasting the warm, buttered sourdough bread. As soon as I had a bite, I wanted more. When we enter the sanctuary, our senses are aroused when we taste the bread and wine representative of Christ's body and blood, when we hear the music that accompanies boisterous singing, when we touch the shoulder of a friend in need of prayer, and when we see the varying generations gathered to worship God. The more we taste, smell, see, and touch, the more we will desire for the church's presence to take priority.

4

Finding the "Right" Local Church

I lamented with a friend not long ago who admitted that she and her family tried to find the "right" church for so long that they decided to just give up looking for the time being. Each church they visited had an issue. The best one was too far, the second on the list had a preacher who was only "OK," another had all the right elements, but the youth group wasn't big enough. Conceding to not being able to find a home church that worked for her family, she defeatedly said, "family devotions will have to do for now."

Here's the reality: *there is no perfect church.* There's not. It doesn't exist. Churches are started, run, and governed by sinners, and every Sunday, they open their doors to more sinners. Christ knows this, which is why He put Himself as the head, and why He made Himself the foundation. The church stands on Him, and it is always about His gospel. If a church steers away from that, there will be significant problems. But even with the constant refocusing, brokenness remains in the ins and outs of our local churches.

The problem with attempting to find the church that checks all the boxes perfectly is that we will be searching indefinitely. If we trust what the Bible says about the priority of the church in our lives, then we need to make every effort to find a church home that preaches and teaches the Bible faithfully, no matter how imperfect the other elements may seem.

For many, finding a home church becomes an issue when they relocate or start college in a new town. I suggest searching for a Bible-believing church as soon as a move is even considered. Of all the factors we consider when choosing a college or an area in which to settle, the surrounding church options don't often make the list. We just figure that we'll settle somewhere and then find a church that works. Prayerfully consider the churches in the area *as part of your decision process,* and not simply after the decision is made. Use the internet to do a search, or ask someone you might know, including a trusted pastor, about solid churches in the area.

When searching for a church to call "home" for you or for family, there are a few important aspects to consider.

Personal Preferences

You may find that some of your "strong" preferences are not found in churches within your area, but if they are just a matter of personal taste and not aspects of worship that are explicit in Scripture, then this is an area where you might need to bend a bit. And what is a "personal preference?" It is the where, when, and how of putting into practice something that is biblically required. For instance, churches need to observe the sacraments but the frequency of that observance or the style of receiving is not explicitly commanded in Scripture. If you tend toward contemporary worship, as another example, but the church nearest to you with solid preaching of the Scripture tends more toward traditional worship, then maybe you lean in for a while and see if this style of worship doesn't grow on you. If you prefer a later service, but the church you're considering only has a 9am, remember that patterns can be adapted and changed. So, while our personal preferences play a part, they are not necessarily determinative for the church you choose.

Biblical Essentials

What is foundational are the aspects of the local church that are explicit in Scripture. Listen to a few sermons and see if the pastor preaches the gospel of Jesus Christ. Are they bold in preaching straight from the Bible? Expository preaching is important, which means that the content of the Scripture passage shapes the sermon, and not the other way around. If you hear a text read but the text is never meaningfully interacted with in a sermon, that might be a red flag. It's dangerous to sit under a preacher who exhorts from his personal opinions rather than what the Scripture teaches.

Take a close look at the leadership of the church, and how the church chooses these leaders. Does their process of selecting, vetting, training and electing church leaders fall in line with such passages as 1 Timothy 3, 1 Peter 5, Titus 1:5-9, and other places where the New Testament provides instruction on church leadership?

And does the church have a general feel of love in its midst? Look, you're not going to find a congregation that does this perfectly, but visit a few times, and see what the *general feel* is, based not just on who smiles at you, but on the actions of the church at large. The Bible exhorts the church over and over to show each other love in word *and* in action. Do you sense this kind of love in your midst? Do their ministries reveal the importance of discipleship and sharpening of one another? And look through the outreach ministries to see if that love extends beyond the church walls.

Pray Earnestly

James 1:5 reminds us that if we need wisdom, we should go to God who will give it to us generously. Don't make a decision regarding a church home without prayerfully considering where the Lord would have you serve Him. Pray regularly and watch to see how the Lord brings clarity, perhaps in unexpected ways.

Most of the Western world is free to attend church anywhere, and this is a freedom we should not take for granted. Many of our brothers and sisters around the world put their life on the line to simply attend a weekly church service. But we are free to worship; we are *not free* to decide *not* to invest in a local church. It's not an option the Bible gives believers. And here's what's beautiful. In His establishment of it, God made the local church to act as an extended family, which can be a tremendous blessing, especially in times of need.

In Acts 20:28, Paul says to the Ephesian Elders, "Pay careful attention to yourselves and to all the flock, in which the Holy Spirit has made you overseers, to care for the church of God, which he obtained with his own blood." Jesus means for us as the church of Christ to watch out for one another, encourage each other, and to love our brother in Christ as if he were our own blood relative. Jesus loves His bride, the church, with such intensity that He shed His blood for her. The question is not, "Where is the perfect church?" but, "How can I involve myself in an imperfect church for the betterment of the flock?"

Be encouraged, child of God. Because of Jesus' death and resurrection, you are a member of this family. The church is a gift, and even with all its imperfections, it is something remarkable to belong to the body of Christ. If you're longing for a child, your life is not void of precious children who need you and look up to you. If you are missing a father or mother, you are not without a spiritual parent who is watching out for you. And if you are a grieving widow, you're not walking this life alone, but you have a family to sustain you, love you, and provide for you. Praise be to Jesus for the gift of His church.

5

Should I Stay or Should I Go?
Reasons to Leave a Local Church

"I can't worship here anymore." The congregant sat with an angry disposition in my husband's office. My husband was the lead pastor at the time, and this congregant had already complained multiple times about our use of drums in the worship service. When my husband tried to explain this was a matter of personal preference, this person pushed back, arguing that the drums are used in places of entertainment, and they cannot and should not be used for worship. This individual appreciated the preaching and grew spiritually because of it, loved our vision and mission, and were grateful for the children's and youth ministry. But those dang drums. He couldn't get over the drums, and so he left.

To be clear, sometimes departing from a church because of conscience-bound convictions may be the right thing to do, and we can trust the Spirit to guide us in this matter. There are certainly other good reasons to leave a church, but I caution anyone who is a member of a church body to leave prayerfully, as a last resort, and not over one area of personal preference.

If you are in a church for any length of time, there is bound to be at least one thing that you become frustrated with. Whether it's a changed policy or a decision made by the leadership, there will eventually be something that rubs you the wrong way. What we must be careful to not do is use manipulative language ("I'm looking at other churches until you make a change in my favor") or just leave entirely over something that could be talked through or that may not be very significant in the long run.

The Bible doesn't address the exact reasons to leave; in fact, many of Paul's letters are written to struggling churches in order to bring restoration and to warn of the many temptations that threaten the unity of a Christian body. However, there are a few biblical reasons to leave a church. Lengthy books have been written on the subject, so this is not meant to be exhaustive, but to highlight just a few of the main reasons, according to Scripture, to leave a church.

1. *False Teaching (Gal. 1:7-9).* If a preacher is preaching or teaching a false gospel, then flee. Twisting the words of Scripture ultimately denies the sufficiency of Jesus, and this is deeply problematic. There is no reason to hesitate in leaving a church that is incorporating false teaching. One word of caution, however. If your pastor says something that you *think* sounds like false teaching but is uncharacteristic of his teaching or preaching, it's going to be in your best interest to talk with him and see if you can gain clarity and insight as to what the pastor intended. It might be that you misunderstood, or it might that the pastor simply did not communicate the point well. If, however, you discover that the pastor intentionally said something that is indeed heretical or not in accordance with the Word of God, it is time to find a new church home.

2. *The sacraments are not biblically upheld (Matt. 28:18-20; Matt. 26:26-29).* If a church is not practicing baptism or the Lord's Supper, or if they are doing it out of accord with what the Scripture teaches, this is a reason to find another church home as the sacraments are biblically mandated.

3. *The peace of the church is threatened (Rom. 16:17).* There are varying examples of this, but if church leaders exhibit

or tolerate abusive behavior or turn a blind eye to those in the congregation blatantly causing dissension or disruption, this may be a reason to leave.

4. *The church discounts discipline and/or membership (Heb. 13:17, 1 Tim. 5:17; 1 Cor. 5:1-12).* If church membership is unimportant to a church, then there is no accountability for the congregants. And if there is no accountability then a church will gradually devolve into something less than a church, as has been witnessed in many mainline churches over the years. These are difficult and sensitive matters, but they cannot be ignored in Scripture.

Here's the bottom line. There is so much church-hopping in Evangelical churches, and a lot of it happens for reasons that are, frankly, insufficient. After serving in the church with my husband for nearly twenty-five years, I know how complicated this issue can be, but we've got to slow down the process and re-examine the reasons why we're leaving. Are they just personal preference? Are our reasons purely selfish? Is it something that, with patience, we might be able to reconsider?

Children and youth ministries are the most frequent reasons people give when leaving a church. Understand that if you leave because of a better children's ministry elsewhere or a bigger youth group somewhere different, you will likely be tempted to leave again when these ministries no longer directly affect you. We also must be careful with having a consumerist mindset when it comes to staying in our churches. Early on in a church we planted, a family left to attend a church with a bigger youth group. We tried to explain that we needed them for our group to grow – in these kinds of ministries, numbers increase numbers! But they weren't interested in being a part of the building process.

I understand this is difficult as I have walked through these challenges with our own young children and teens, but we can't allow our kids to be the ones who spiritually direct our household. We also should not leave a church with whom we have covenanted in order to be "better served" elsewhere. This is an incredibly consumeristic approach and misses the purpose of the church altogether. Children and youth ministries are significant, and both are later addressed in this book, so let's find ways to serve them and enhance them in our local churches rather than leaving good churches to find better student ministries elsewhere.

If you are leaving a local congregation, be sure you have made your decision slowly and only after having had a conversation with the pastor or other leadership (they are deserving of this), spending significant time in prayer, and being honest with yourself and with God as to whether your decision is consumeristic or biblical.

PART TWO:
Engaging in Corporate Worship

Oh come, let us sing to the Lord;
let us make a joyful noise to the rock of our salvation!
Let us come into his presence with thanksgiving;
let us make a joyful noise to him with songs of praise!
For the Lord is a great God,
and a great King above all gods.

Psalm 95:1-3

My parents passed away at fairly young ages, but they left a life-long imprint, especially in their passion for corporate worship. Each week, my dad was regularly and sincerely excited to attend Sunday morning church. I remember standing in the kitchen on many occasions debriefing a unique church service over a bowl of ice-cream. I can picture his smile as his arms widened when he expressed how much he loved it when the music "got big!"

I'm the music director at our church, and by the grace of God alone, I feel this same kind of excitement most Sundays. The elements of a service can be spiritually enhancing, and even awe-inspiring if we allow the Lord to open our hearts to the unique beauty of corporate worship.

6

Attending Worship Even When You Don't Have It All Together

When my kids were little, Sunday mornings were one of the most hectic mornings of the week, and as a pastor's wife, I was solo in getting the kids to church in their early days. Simply getting them dressed felt like a great feat. One Sunday we were running very late, not at all unusual for this stage in my life, and I was scheduled to play piano for the church service. When I went to gather my youngest, about four years old at the time, she was still in her pj's. Frantically, I told my child to get dressed quickly and get in the car immediately.

At some point, my youngest sauntered into the back seat of the car without any of us noticing her clothes. Once we were all in the vehicle, I made the mad dash to church. I was just about to congratulate myself on only being five minutes late when my oldest muttered, "Um, mom. Have you seen what Lily is wearing?" I adjusted the rear-view mirror and stared in horror at my four-year-old who was wearing a pillowcase. She had cut a larger hole, just big enough for her head, and made two small slits perfectly suited for her little arms to slip through. *For Sunday morning church, my daughter was dressed in bedding.* I trudged into worship feeling defeated and frenzied, holding the hand of my little girl dressed in a torn and fringed pillowcase.

My guess is that many walk into church on a Sunday morning feeling a bit frantic. Others enter with a kind of spiritual fog surrounding them, and some come feeling a real resistance because of deep frustrations with others in the church body. Believer, no matter what you are feeling or what the circumstances were that preceded your attendance, what is important is that you come.

The Lord does not ask us to enter His presence when we have it all together. No. He says to come into His presence with thanksgiving and a heart ready to make a joyful noise to Him (Ps. 95). No matter what our week or morning entailed, believers in Jesus have reason to come into corporate worship *with thankful hearts.*

We are there, freely, to worship our great God, the great King above all gods (Ps. 95:3), the One who holds in His hands the deepest places of the earth and the highest hills known to man (Ps. 95:4). We come to worship our Creator, the One who spoke the sea into existence and formed the dry land we walk on (Ps. 95:5), but who is also our Abba Father, and who tenderly watches over every detail of our life. For these reasons, we should come regularly with hearts ready to burst with thanksgiving for who God is and for all He has done. When our hearts feel the least ready to worship is usually when our soul needs it the most.

We shouldn't wait until we *feel* ready to come to worship. Most weeks we simply would not attend, but we come, imperfect, with gratitude in our heart, ready and willing to worship our sovereign God who penned the details of our week, both the hardship and the joys, for our good and for His glory (Rom. 8:28). Come as you are because you serve a great God who has done great things, and who is worthy of your honor and gladly receives your feeble praise.

7

Preparing Our Heart for Worship

One of the ways we can get the most out of worship is by preparing for it ahead of time. People do this with almost every other area that they deem important. Whether it's a sporting event or a job interview, we prepare for what we're excited about and what we anticipate. We should treat corporate worship with the same kind of eagerness, and in doing so, prepare our minds and hearts for Sunday morning. What often happens instead is that we treat worship like we are a spectator, waiting to see what it can do for us, rather than an active engager, making every effort to get the most out of our time in God's house.

We're not passive spectators in worship; we're active participants, and active engagement requires meaningful preparation. Consider a few practical ways to prepare for Sunday morning worship:

1. *Read the sermon passage as a family.* Many struggle with what to do for family devotions, especially when kids get older, so find out what passage will be preached on, and then read and discuss various parts of it. This will only enhance the preaching of God's Word. The times I have put this into practice, I've found myself eager to learn more about certain verses that may seem obscure or confusing.

2. *Listen to the songs that will be sung.* Some churches make the details of the worship service available before Sunday morning. If this is the case, create a playlist of songs and hymns that will be sung and play the arrangements

throughout the week. This kind of preparation helps the words of songs become especially meaningful after dwelling on them more than once.

3. *Pray.* This really should become a priority for every believer anticipating worship on a Sunday morning. Spend time praying that the Lord will bind Satan with all his creative Sunday morning tactics and allow you to be free from distraction. Pray for your leaders. Pray that your attitude will edify others. Pray for the brother and sister who you will stand next to in worship. Pray for the children who will be present and pray that the Lord will be glorified in every word that is spoken and every note that is played. Prepare to meet the Lord in *His* sanctuary. He is worthy of the extra time, and our worship will be enriched because of it.

8

Worship By Singing

As a worship director, one of my greatest weekly joys is hearing God's people sing. In fact, each time we debrief a service, my first question is: *Did the congregation sing boldly?* If you can speak, you can sing! And singing is not a suggested form of worship, but it's an assumed and commanded part of worship: "O come, let us sing to the Lord; let us make a joyful noise to the rock of our salvation!" (Ps. 95:1). There are hundreds of references to singing in the Bible, and over fifty direct commandments to SING.

Jesus sings! He grew up singing the Psalms with God's people, and in the gospels, it's documented that Jesus sang hymns (Matt. 26:30). God Himself sings. Zephaniah 3:17 says that He exalts over His beloved with "loud singing." I often wonder what God's singing voice sounds like. Thunder? A chorus of angels? I don't know, but I love to imagine it. And the times in my life when congregational singing sweeps me up, even moving me to tears, are the times when I'm reminded how much greater the singing voice of God must be, and I can't wait to hear it someday.

We are created in the image of God, so we are made to be singers as God is a singer, and in doing so, we bring glory to the One who gave us our breath. And Jesus receives our sincere worship as a sweet fragrance of offering. I know there are many who tend to stand silent during congregational singing because they feel uncomfortable or awkward. But know that the Lord is not looking for perfect pitches or great harmonies, and He will help us in our insecurities. Have you considered asking the Lord to help you with the command to sing in corporate worship? The psalmist recognizes His need for Jesus and says, "I lift my eyes to the hills, where does my help come from?" Our help, in any circumstance, comes from the One who made the hills, the One who made you, the One who created you to sing.

And when we lift our voice in song, our personal relationship with Jesus is strengthened. Singing bends our souls to God. When we enter the sanctuary confused or hurt, we can sing through our tears and weakened voice, "In Christ ALONE my hope is found…" finding healing in the reminder that our hope is in Jesus. When we come with hearts overflowing with joy, we can respond in gratitude singing boldly to the one from whom all blessings flow, "Then sings my soul, My Savior God, to Thee, how great Thou art!"

But singing not only strengthens our relationship with Jesus, it also strengthens the bond between believers. In Colossians 3, Paul reminds the church that one of the ways their relationship with one another is strengthened is through song: "And above all these put on love, which binds everything together in perfect harmony … And be thankful. Let the word of Christ dwell in you richly, teaching and admonishing one another in all wisdom, singing psalms and hymns and spiritual songs, with thankfulness in your hearts to God."

What is profoundly beautiful is that when we sing in worship, we all become members of a choir singing together to our King. What else is more unifying than to sing the same words of confession or adoration with those in differing stages and places in life? It's very easy to slip into making worship about us, and when that happens, we may become self-conscious when another sees us singing or lifting our hands in praise, but when worship is about coming together to praise our Savior, then smiles from across the sanctuary while singing become sweet reminders of the bond we have forever through Jesus.

One of the greatest gifts of congregational singing is that it makes the truths that we know intellectually sink deep into our hearts. It is a very different experience to simply recite the words, "It is well, it is well with my soul," than to sing these words with the melodies they were given. And the lyrics we sing sit in our heart in a unique way, moving us, whether we realize it or not, into a deeper understanding of Scriptural truths. As singer/songwriter Keith Getty says, "Singing takes Sunday's truths into Monday morning." Come. Worship. And Sing. Sing out to your great God giving praise to Him for who He is and giving thanks to Him for all He has done.

9

Worship Through Confession

There's not often a lot of silence in worship. Some churches don't include it at all, but many incorporate a few moments of corporate or silent confession in each worship service. But we're so feeble. Even if the sanctuary is void of momentary sound to allow for personal confession, our own wavering thoughts convert the silence, almost instantly, to moments that feel awkward, confusing, *even loud.*

Sometimes this happens because we haven't taken to heart the connection between confession and worship. As important as it is for us to enter worship with thanksgiving ready to praise God with our singing, it is just as significant to look forward to a time of reflection and contrition before our great God.

The prophet Isaiah closes his book with this promise from God in Isaiah 66:1-2:

> Thus says the Lord: 'Heaven is my throne, and the earth is my footstool; what is the house that you would build for me, and what is the place of my rest? All these things my hand has made, and so all these things came to be, declares the Lord. But this is the one to whom I will look: he who is humble and contrite in spirit and trembles at my word.

God is not so concerned that we simply show up to worship, but that we worship Him with a heart that is humble and repentant. If we view our sin as something small or insignificant, that's the view we will have of our Savior. One of the factors that enables our worship, that causes sincere singing to our King, is a deep understanding of how great our sin is, and how much we need God's forgiveness. Some churches have removed this time of reflection because it can make churchgoers (and visitors) uncomfortable. And yet, one of the most crucial elements of effective worship is an understanding that God is perfectly holy, and we are not. We must cling to Him for forgiveness and acknowledgement of our sin. If we do not see the *necessity* of this time during a church service, then our worship of Jesus may be hindered. When we bow our head silently amid a room filled with God's children, we are reminded that we are not alone in our sin; and when we utter words of confession corporately, we are affirming to one another that we are together, as a body of believers, seeking to put sin to death. You are not alone with your sin; thanks be to God.

I talked recently with a friend who said that for her, confession is one of the main draws to attending church consistently: "Think about it. How many times in the regular work week do you actually stop, bow your head, and have a concentrated time of confession." To have this time carved out weekly as a sort of recalibration for our spiritual lives is essential and formative in our relationship with Jesus. My friend's husband added that confession is like a horse race. Prior to the acknowledgement of our sin before God, we're like the horse and jockey who are hindered from moving forward because of the swinging doors blocking them from the track. But after we openly and honestly confess our sins before God, we can run through those doors with joy, uninhibited and free from the weight caused by our sin.

Confession, whether it's silent or corporately spoken, awakens our soul because it opens our eyes to the grace and mercy of our Savior. This time in worship should never feel rote or mundane, and if it does, ask the Lord to open your eyes to whatever indwelling sin might be keeping you from sincere confession before Him. This can be a difficult thing to pray, but it's necessary for us to worship freely and earnestly.

And if you tend to avoid leaning into confession because you feel too ashamed, know that there is forgiveness – completely and freely – in the name of Jesus. In Psalm 51, David offers his personal confession after committing adultery with Bathsheba and murdering her husband. When David is confronted with his sin and realizes the magnitude of what he has done, he immediately draws near to God knowing that God will wash him whiter than snow (v. 7), that He will lift him out of his pain and restore his joy and gladness (v. 8), and that his God will show him mercy and steadfast love (v. 1). But to get to this point of worshipful restoration, believer, we must first acknowledge the depth of our sin and then confess it to our God.

John 6:37 says, " … whoever comes to me I will never cast out." What refreshing and beautiful words. God bridged the gap between Himself and sinners when Christ died on the cross. The more time we spend in deep reflection of our sin, the greater we will see the span of the arms that hung on the cross. Our love for worship grows immensely as we become more aware of our indwelling sin and the debt that was paid that we might be free of it. The next time a quiet time of reflection is offered in a service or a corporate prayer of confession is included in the worship, confess your sins to our great God who washes them away by His blood. And then notice the heartfelt and deep praise that follows as you give thanks to the One who covers you with His unending, unrelenting grace.

10

Worship by Hearing and Responding to God's Word

When I was young, my mom used to pack cheerios and a sticker book to keep me occupied during Sunday church, and specifically, during the sermon. We didn't sit with our parents on Sunday mornings; my dad was the preacher, and my mom sang in the choir. So, we sat with family friends who acted as surrogates and told me when to sit and when to stand, and many times over, when to be quiet.

To the dismay of others, I didn't mind the singing part. I innocently sang the songs at the top of my lungs, unaware of anyone else around me. But I distinctly remember my sticker books. As soon as dad stood at the pulpit, the cheerios came out (I ate each one slowly and methodically, trying to make them last through the *whole, long sermon),* and the sticker book was opened. I remember getting in trouble one Sunday because of "scratch and sniff" stickers. I suppose the sniff didn't produce a strong enough smell because I scratched so hard that I became a distraction to those around me.

What I don't remember in those early years is my dad's preaching. But that changed over time. There wasn't some dramatic moment when all the sudden the sermons began to "click," but as I grew in my understanding of who Jesus is, and as I learned more about what the Bible says, the sermons started to become something of great interest to me. This is a natural process for every believer because as we grow in our faith, a process called sanctification, what we hear preached from

God's Word becomes more and more significant as the divine nourishment contributes to our spiritual growth. Conversely, when we're not regularly exposed to the preaching of God's Word, our spiritual growth can become stunted.

When we come to worship in our local churches, it is expected that part of the worship experience is hearing the Word of God and responding to it with our minds (Ps. 119:113), and our hearts (Ps. 119:2), and the more this happens, the faster we grow out of our child-like mentality toward the preaching of the Word and into a disposition of longing for it. By the grace of God, we even become hungry for the preaching and teaching, needing it weekly for our soul's sustenance. I love the passage in Ezekiel 3 when God tells Ezekiel to "eat the scroll" (3:1) or internalize and digest the Word of God before declaring it to the Israelites. The prophet obeys saying, "Then I ate it, and it was in my mouth as sweet as honey" (v. 3). As the words fill his body in this vision, there was a sense of satisfaction – Ezekiel could only describe the digesting of God's words with the sweetest thing he could imagine.

In Psalm 19, David describes God's Word with the same kind of sweetness: "sweeter also than honey and drippings of the honeycomb" (v. 10). The Psalmist sets out to describe the Scriptures in Psalm 19 using parallelism – six nouns to explain what the Bible is, six adjectives to describe it, and six verbs to encourage believers with the incredible effect that God's Word can have. Look at the remarkable adjectives David uses to describe the Bible: perfect, sure, right, pure, clean, and true. How could you not hunger for something that is *all six of these of these words all the time*? And when we immerse ourselves in Scripture, the Psalmist affirms that it affects us immensely: God's Word revives our soul, makes us wise, gives us joy, enlightens our eyes, it endures forever, and provides rich blessing in this life.

But one of the greatest benefits of learning from the Bible is that God Himself speaks to us through it, teaching us more about who He is. When we begin to grasp the magnificence of this, the sermon on a Sunday can produce life-altering change. When a pastor faithfully preaches from the Word of God, the Spirit works both in the minister as he explains and applies, and in the congregation, as they listen and respond.

If you are blessed to have a pastor whose preaching style connects with you, give thanks to God for this. But even good and godly pastors will, every so often, give sermons that fall flat to a listener's ears. This is not a new issue in the church. In fact, John Newton, author of "Amazing Grace", was also a pastor, and a congregant once described his preaching as "utterance [that was] far from clear, and his attitudes ungraceful."[1] But here's the thing. People still filled the sanctuary each Sunday to hear him. And why? Because Newton faithfully preached the Word, because he loved his congregants, and because the Holy Spirit worked in and amongst both Newton and his church-goers. You see, our ability to learn from God's Word is *not solely dependent on the preacher*. Don't think so highly of a mere man! Your ability to be pierced by God's Word is the work of the Spirit in you, and it is the work of the Spirit as the preacher proclaims His Word. As stated before, the power of God's Spirit is mighty. The Spirit that is at work when the Scriptures are opened is the same One who raised Jesus from the dead. *That is powerful.* So, ask that Spirit to open your heart and your mind to His Word, and watch and see how the Lord increases your appetite for the Scriptures no matter the style of the pastor.

If you are sitting under a preacher with whom you do not connect, but who still faithfully preaches God's Word, before you flee the body in search of a better preacher, or rant about his shortcomings to others around you, consider a few important

---

1. Works of John Newton (Edinburgh: Banner of Truth Trust, 2015), 1:CX

reminders. First, to preach week in and week out is weighty, and most pastors prepare a sermon feeling that weight and knowing that they will inevitably fall short. Second, we must be realistic with the expectations we have of our pastors. The entertainment industry has so skewed our views and attention spans that we have unrealistic expectations of being "wooed" or "ahhed" every time the preacher steps into the pulpit. That's not the preacher's job, though he is often preaching to a group who expects far beyond what is his primary calling on a Sunday morning. And lastly, we must be as prayerful for our own hearts as we are for our pastors who open God's Word for us. Pray that your heart will soften to the preaching of the Word and pray that God will bind Satan so that what has been revealed to the pastor by God's Spirit is also readily received by God's people.

It's also important to remember that we can't be merely listeners of God's Word. We also have a responsibility to actively respond to it. Psalm 95 is an exuberant invitation to come and worship the Lord, but it ends with a very stark reminder for those who do not listen to God's Word with obedient ears. It's easy to listen and respond when life is plodding along in the way we planned. It's more difficult to respond obediently when we are convicted by His Word and forced to trust when we don't understand the path God has chosen for us.

Verse 8 of Psalm 95 warns the believer: "Today, if you hear his voice, do not harden your hearts, as at Meribah, as on the day at Massah in the wilderness." At Meribah and Massah, the Israelites argued and complained, forgetting that God promised to deliver them. Oh, how quickly they forgot God's faithfulness and His goodness. He delivered them from slavery, He kept them from the plagues, and He even parted the Red Sea for them to safely cross. Though He proved faithful, though He promised deliverance, God's words fell on deaf ears because they did not respond to their wandering in obedience but in bitterness.

It's important that we come into His presence, humbly asking that the Lord will open our heart to hear His Word and respond to it with faith, even when we don't fully understand it. The Bible makes no mistakes, and even though many of its words are not popular in our current culture, we can trust it because it was written for us by the Creator of the Universe. Hear the Word of our great God, give praise to Him by responding to it obediently, and give thanks to the One who inspired its perfect and trustworthy words.

11

Cultivating a Love for Worship in Young Children

When my youngest was about seven, I decided it was time to help her become more engaged in the worship service. Because she liked to doodle, I bought her a journal and some pens and told her it might be easier to listen to the sermon if she writes down some of what the pastor talked about. Perhaps she could draw a picture of what he read from the Bible or write down a question she might have.

The next Sunday, she opened her new journal with a sense of enthusiasm when the sermon began. The pens were moving voraciously, and my heart swelled with pride. She was listening and learning! I couldn't wait to see how her young heart responded to God's Word, so when the service ended and she hurried off to ensure she was the first in line at the snack table, I opened the journal and read this story:

> I was eating my cheeseburger. I could taste the cheesy chicken and bread. It was time for class, but Bob tripped me. I punched Bob, so the teacher sent me to the principal.
> I tried to tell her, but the principal said I was in trouble.

The made-up story was followed by an elaborate picture… of Bob. I still have the page from her journal nestled in my Bible, serving as a humble reminder that ultimately, God does the work in my child's spiritual life. And yet, we still have a role as parents and spiritual parents in passing down a love for worship to the next generation. God is in complete control, and He has lovingly written their stories, of which many of us will be a part because of what we said, taught, or modeled for our children.

For younger kids, they learn so much by example; they're impacted simply by watching and observing what happens within their own context. As a young child, I observed several holidays where my mom would switch out our entire cabinet of everyday dishes and replace them with ones that displayed holly and other festive decorations. When I went to a friends' house one afternoon during Christmas time, I asked why they were using their "normal" dishes. I just assumed that what I observed from my mom was a norm for everyone, and for a brief time in my own adult life, I even carried on this laborious tradition.

Because our kids are so influenced by our example, simply modeling for them an eagerness for the rhythms of a worship service helps cultivate a love for it in their own heart. If you're embarrassed to sing, don't think that your kids won't catch on. Or if you sing out in the car, but remain silent in the sanctuary, don't assume they won't follow your example. *Show* them what it is to sing heartfelt praise, to humbly confess, and to listen intently as the Scripture is read.

And talk about the service with your children. Sunday lunch or Monday devotions are good times to take advantage of talking about the service, and not just by asking, "What did you learn?" but for our young kids, help them to reminisce corporate worship with all their senses: What did you see? What did you feel? Did you smell anything? To that question, you may get a giggle or a silly answer, but your kids may also surprise you. For Lent one year, our church members each wrote a sin they were struggling with on a rock. The rocks were gathered and put in one large pile that eventually sprouted flowers on Easter Sunday. The week we created the pile of rocks, a child from our congregation said to me, "I smell rocks, which means I smell my sin." It was a child-like response, yes, but he was using his senses to make spiritual connections, and it was beautiful.

Since our children learn by example, they will also pick up on the value that you and your family place on worship. If we believe the church should be a priority, that it's centrality in our families is significant, then we need to follow through with consistency in Sunday worship. If you are regularly missing corporate worship with a child because of an extra-curricular event or because you're too tired to get there most weeks, then we can't expect that our children will grow into adults who make worship a priority. If worship is just one of many activities to pick from on a Sunday morning, that's a difficult pattern to break the older a child becomes. Instead, make corporate worship a life liturgy for your child, even if it means sacrificing another Sunday morning event. The blessing that comes from the regular rhythm of corporate worship is real and tangible, and when it becomes the norm, it's *missed* when you're not able to be there. But when families don't attend regularly, the hunger for worship tends to diminish.

And as you approach the weekend, talk with as much vigor about the upcoming worship service as you do your child's soccer game or gymnastics meet. Do you ask questions in preparation for worship like you would another event that your child is excited to attend? The Lord has set aside one day a week for us to rest and worship; one day a week for us to stand with our extended family giving praise and glory to our maker, so we should do what we can, by the grace of God, to cultivate an environment in our homes that eagerly anticipates meeting God in His house on the Lord's Day.

And young moms and dads, I want to encourage you specifically in your efforts to bring your sweet babies and toddlers to church. You may go through half of box of cheerios to keep them quiet. You may end up chasing them, bouncing them, and bringing them in and out of the service all while wondering why you even made the effort. But even when it's hard, keep bringing them to worship. They see you sing; they watch you bow your head in prayer, and they are learning, even before they can talk, the daily rhythms of life by watching you chase after Jesus and learn to love His church. Bring them to worship. The season of life when it seems it is not worth it is the most important time to get your children to church.

It should be the prayer of every member in a church that the children who run the hallways and scour the snack table eventually fall in love with worshipping God corporately. Pray unceasingly that your child's heart will bend toward their creator and that they will grow to anticipate the worship of this great God who loves them abundantly more than we ever could or ever will.

12

Cultivating a Love for Worship in Teens

It wasn't long ago that I sat with a friend who expressed the hard reality that her teenager no longer wanted to attend church. "Do I make him go?" she asked sincerely. Prior to having teenagers myself, I probably would have said, "By all means. Put down your foot, mom!" But I have too much first-hand experience with teenage resistance, and it's not as black and white as we might have thought it was when they were little and had no choice but to follow us in tow. In the early years I'd put my toddler in the car seat, and she'd innocently ask, "Where are we going, Momma?" They followed without choice, and in many cases without concern as to where we were headed.

When they're teenagers, this is not often the case. We can't just strap them in, and they don't always willingly follow our lead. A teen not wanting to attend church is a familiar battle to many, and as the earlier statistics confirm, it will likely remain a battle for the next generation. Parents of teens, we need to both empathize but also exhort because whether your child has professed faith in Jesus or not, they need corporate worship.

First, it's important to empathize with your teen. If you grew up in the church, certainly you remember Sundays that you didn't want to get up and go. Or perhaps there's a deeper, relational reason they don't want to attend. Or maybe they've just decided they don't believe what is being preached, and they view the church body as one big mass of hypocrites. These are all reasons I've heard from young people as to why they don't want to attend church. Hear them out. When your teen expresses resistance, ask questions. Do more listening than responding and try to hear where their heart really is. What is underlying their resistance to attend? Listening well and showing empathy will guide any needed exhortation.

As parents, we can take comfort in knowing that our children's salvation and their love for the church is not dependent on us. You can breathe a sigh of relief because *you don't save your child.* It is by grace they are saved, the same grace that you and I experienced the moment that we gave our lives to the Lord. But this does not mean that we don't bear responsibility for our child's spiritual growth. Deuteronomy 6 is one place that makes this clear:

"You shall love the Lord your God with all your heart and with all your soul and with all your might ... You shall teach them diligently to your children, and shall talk of them when you sit in your house, and when you walk by the way, and when you rise. You shall bind them as a sign on your hand, and they shall be as frontlets between your eyes. You shall write them on the doorposts of your house and on your gates" (v. 4-9).

You *shall* teach the love of the Lord as diligently and consistently as possible, and in the strength of the Lord. You don't have these difficult conversations on your own. Child of God, you are *in Christ,* and because of that, you have His wisdom, His strength, His grace, His understanding. He is right there with you when you are seeking to guide your teen.

And one of the greatest ways we can teach the love of God is through the worship of Him. When a child is living under your roof, one of the expectations should be to attend corporate worship with the family. That doesn't mean that they must agree with everything or that they must believe what you believe – we can't make them do that – but we can expect that they go.

But as you get closer to launching them into the world, it may be that soon before they leave the nest, you release this expectation, giving them the freedom to choose whether they attend worship. Perhaps you'll be pleasantly surprised that they go, even if out of habit. But you may find that with this kind of freedom, they stop attending altogether. Be encouraged in God's perfect sovereignty in their life and use the time to talk about their choice *before* they leave the nest. This can be incredibly beneficial, equipping them with biblical truths and considerations to ponder before they leave and begin setting new patterns for themselves.

Pray for your teen's experience in corporate worship. Pray that they might be loved by another brother or sister, even someone they sit next to during the service. Pray that their hearts will be open to the gospel, pray that God will reveal to them their sin and need for a Savior, pray that the singing of God's people will inspire worship, and then trust. Trust in the Lord with all your heart and lean not on your own understanding (Prov. 3:5). The Lord is at work, and He loves your teen more than you can ever comprehend; He reveals Himself, in powerful ways, when we come together to worship Him in His house. Trust this. We serve a great God who does great wonders for His people, including our beloved teens. He is worthy of our praise.

PART THREE:
Involvement in the Church's Ministries: The Importance of Connection

And they devoted themselves to the apostles' teaching and the fellow-ship, to the breaking of bread and the prayers. And awe came upon every soul, and many wonders and signs were being done through the apostles. And all who believed were together and had all things in common. And they were selling their possessions and belongings and distributing the proceeds to all, as any had need. And day by day, attending the temple together and breaking bread in their homes, they received their food with glad and generous hearts, praising God and having favor with all the people. And the Lord added to their number day by day those who were being saved.

Acts 2:42-47

13

Why Connect?

While preaching on a Sunday morning, my husband watched as one church member followed his very typical Sunday morning pattern. Each week he arrived late and slipped out early, just when he sensed that the sermon was nearing its end. After noticing this pattern for several months, my husband asked the congregant about it. He said quite matter-of-factly, "All I need is the weekly sermon, and I'm good." My husband was taken aback by his answer, but I think many function with this mindset. They may not all arrive late or leave early, but one hour on a Sunday morning sounds just about right for many churchgoers today. In fact, one or two hours just twice a month might do the trick.

Believer in Christ, this is not what God intended for His church. You will often hear church leaders press into the idea of church involvement, and most do not do this for any other reason than that they know the church will better fulfill its ideal in loving one another and proclaiming the gospel message of Jesus if they are *connected*. Your involvement in your church matters, whatever the size, and whatever your stage of life.

In the book of Acts we find the church in Paul's day loving on one other, serving one another, stirring each other up to do good works, and providing for the needs of one another (Acts 2:42-47). What this means it that the church – as a group of people – were together, and they were connected to one another. It says in Acts 4:32, this early church was "one in heart and mind." Imagine experiencing that kind of unity! If you've been to a sporting event and sat in the fan section of the team you're rooting for, the comradery amongst the people is oddly intense. All the cheering and chanting and high fiving is a sign of a unified group all desiring the same outcome. In a similar way, when church members are together regularly and understand their purpose and aim, there is a unique sense of oneness amongst the body, exemplifying in many ways the ideal of friendship.

The result of this kind of intense connectedness in the early church was profound. No one was needy among them, and they fulfilled the great commission as they preached the gospel and lived it out amongst one another. They were a witness to the world because of their unity and love for each other. Interestingly, while Luke points out the benefits of the connectedness that the early church had, he also includes the sad story of Ananias and Sapphira who act selfishly, holding back from others in the community, and the result for both is death. The juxtaposition of the flourishing church providing for one another with the selfishness of these two people reveals how seriously God takes the sin that threatens the unity of His church.

As the church continues to establish itself and spread, Paul's interest in their ongoing connectedness and their steadfastness to the gospel message is clear in the letters he sends to these churches. Many of them exhort the believers in the church to *love one another*. That "one another" loving happens within a church body, and it affects the church's witness and the church's togetherness. This tight-knit community under the headship of Christ that was intended for the church can certainly be experienced in varying local churches today, but it is difficult to do so if you are only committed to your church family for an hour on a Sunday morning.

This means that if we are going to find connectedness in our local church, we need to be involved outside of the Sunday morning service. Doing so will likely require some sacrifice on your part. It may mean cutting something in your schedule for the sake of involving yourself in a church ministry, or it may mean sacrificing the comfort of being at home every evening during the week. It may also mean taking a step of faith and getting involved in something outside of your comfort zone. Yes, sacrifice may be required, but the benefits are abundant. Feeling connected in a church body is like coming home to a family that you cannot wait to see. Being loved by a church member is to feel the embrace of your heavenly Father through their tender hug. Connect in, child of God, get involved, and in doing so, experience the profound goodness of knowing and being known by the family of God.

14

Church Involvement for the Super Busy Family

I was a few minutes early to our weekly Bible study when a fellow mom came and sat next to me letting out a defeated sigh. Sensing she was overwhelmed, I asked her if everything was alright. "Yes," she answered apathetically. "I just don't think I can keep coming to this study, though. We are just so super busy right now."

I felt a frustration surface, and not because she might not return, though I knew her presence would be missed. It was because I was overwhelmed as well, and she beat me to the complaining. I showed up that morning feeling utterly overwhelmed from working multiple jobs, trying to finish school, and attempting to meet the needs of my children as best as I was able. I brought mere fumes to the table, but I also lamented that returning the sentiment would only turn into what has become a "typical" Western exchange: "How are you?" "Great; just super busy." "And how are you?" "Good; just also super busy." But I told her anyway, admittedly with an edge to my voice: "Yeah, I'm super busy right now too."

Busyness. Everyone experiences it, in some season or another, because it is inevitable, at least in our Western life. There is work to be done, deadlines to meet, there are people to connect with, children and grandchildren with activities and responsibilities, and then ... there is the church. How can we possibly give *more* time to this body when our plates are already overflowing? I wondered that morning what my friend and I were doing in the study that day. Perhaps, I lamented, our time would be better spent elsewhere. We were both, after all, just really, super busy.

One of the primary reasons people leave a church is because they do not feel connected into a body of believers. During our twenty-five years in ministry, if a family has not relocated, feeling disconnected is the main reason families give for leaving the church or looking elsewhere. If this has been the case for you, it may certainly be due to an unwelcoming community or because of leaders who do not set the precedent for a hospitable environment. But more often than not, the disconnectedness comes from a lack of involvement, and the lack of involvement is usually blamed on a full schedule. You see, our expectation is connectedness. We all want it. But we desire it without having to go above and beyond. But togetherness in a church family doesn't work this way; it does take effort. The reality is, we must find places outside of regular Sunday morning worship to invest in while also managing the ongoings of a *super busy schedule*. Easy, right? Not at all, but let me suggest the first step.

Pastor and writer Kevin DeYoung talks about the "Plus One" approach to the church.[1] The idea is that you make Sunday morning a priority and then think of one more ministry to commit to within your local church setting. I like this approach, especially for those individuals or families who find themselves in unique seasons of busyness. Of course, the "Plus One" approach is meant to get us to the point of feeling connected in a dry season spiritually or a season filled with multiple other responsibilities. The hope and prayer is that, as time goes on, we will continue answering varying calls to serve in the church and involve ourselves in its ministries as time opens and our desire to connect in grows deeper.

---

1. https://www.thegospelcoalition.org/blogs/kevin-deyoung/the-plus-one-approach-to-church/

For super busy families, Sunday worship should remain a priority *no matter what.* During the years that followed the COVID-19 pandemic, we heard about - and watched - church attendance decreasing across the country. On average, those who attended church once-a-month pre-pandemic began attending quarterly; those who attended church twice a month before the pandemic were now about once-a-month attenders, and there was a blatant increase in attenders who did not come because they were tired from a long weekend otherwise and could choose instead the convenience of online worship. Friends, the inconsistency in Sunday worship can weaken your relationship with Jesus and loosen the tight connectedness God desires for you to have with others in His church. Of course, we cannot be legalistic here. Church attendance does not save you, but it does strengthen you spiritually as it nourishes your soul and as it reorients our focus on Jesus. Yes, there will be times we miss a service because of travel or illnesses, but whenever we are able, we should be in worship on a Sunday at our local church. I know this is contrary to our culture where weekend vacation homes are prevalent and sports games on Sunday are unending. Like anything in life, we choose what we prioritize. And prioritizing Sunday worship is the first step toward connectedness. Psalm 92:13 says, "[The Righteous] are planted in the house of the Lord; they flourish in the courts of our God." Those who are faithful in the house of God will flourish like a mighty tree planted in the temple whose roots have grown into the sanctuary. But the rooting – the flourishing – won't happen if you are only there occasionally.

Beyond this, the super busy family should consider picking one other ministry in which to invest. And investing, to be clear, is not showing up when you feel like it or giving an hour of your time once a semester, but investing in a ministry is committing yourself to it, attending or serving it regularly, and sacrificing other activities to remain faithful to it. This might be a Bible study, it might be a small group, a choir, or even a church sports league. It may also be an area of service in your church that needs weekly help such as a food pantry or team that oversees the coffee and snacks on a Sunday morning. Perhaps think about joining the group of greeters at your church – this is another great area of "Plus One" to consider as it provides a built-in opportunity to get to know others who enter the doors on a Sunday morning. A few of these areas of ministry are touched on in the following chapters.

In the mayhem of life, it's not usually sports, dance class, school, work, or socials that become the casualty of the whirlwind that is the busyness of life. It's the church. Most often, it's the people of God who are neglected when we have so much else to do. Believer in Christ, we cannot, and should not, make the church the martyr of our time.

The Bible study that my super busy friend and I attended that morning ended in tears of gratitude for us both. The passage we dug into was unexpectedly needed and unpredictably nourishing for our weary souls. In the whirlwind, we both needed to be anchored in God's Word and be reminded of His precious promises. And in the mayhem, we needed each other. My friend and I lingered, laughing at the fact that the morning began feeling rushed and out of control, and now we sat, praying, settled, stirring up one another toward the good works ahead. We were both *super busy*, and so what we needed more than anything was to connect with Jesus through our church family.

15

Involvement in Small Group Ministries

The Reasoning Behind Small Group Ministries

As previously mentioned, we learn quite a bit about the early church through the New Testament, and mostly from Paul's letters to the churches. The early churches were not large groups of people, but they would meet in small groups (likely around thirty), and while each group varied, they met in homes for worship (Acts 20:20; 1 Cor. 16:19) often relying on the family unit in the church who had the largest space for the group to gather. This is where we get the idea of "house churches" today. Communion would take place around a table, and baptisms would take place with a basin of water, or they would travel as a group to a river for the ceremony. As Christianity grew, so did persecution, so constructing church buildings would have been out of the question as it would have put an obvious target on a group of Christians, so for quite some time they continued to meet as smaller groups in homes. You can imagine the intimacy and connectedness within these groups! With this background, Paul's exhortation to keep from bickering and lean into love seems vital: you simply could not avoid someone with whom you disagreed, so it was important, for the literal sake of the church, that there was deep love for one another and a clear understanding of the gospel message.

The need for smaller groups within a local church body did not become a necessity until much later, and it became a need to maintain the integral and relational connectedness that bleeds into the whole of the congregation. Pastors report that on average, about 44 per cent of their worship attendees are involved in some kind of small group.[1] This number has declined over the last ten years, and trends suggest that it will continue to decline as fewer people see the need for connection in their local church body.

So, why not give up on the idea? Small groups take work and commitment, so is involvement in them really that significant? Yes, and mostly for the sake of love and integration within the body of believers. The false ideology of our day tries to prove that connectedness can occur through a screen. But even secularists push back on this as the world becomes increasingly aware of the danger that comes from not having regular face-to-face interaction in a community in which you are really known.

Experts say that harm from digital life will continue to increase, and they expect it to worsen as the pace of technology change accelerates. As our connectedness through screens increases, distrust in each other will also grow, and faith in institutions will likely decline. This, experts argue, "could deepen already undesirable levels of polarization, cognitive dissonance and public withdrawal from vital discourse."[2]

Whether your church has grown from twenty to fifty or from 500 to 1,500, we must put forth the effort to be a part of a small group ministry to avoid these frightening trends. We already see that discourse over arguable topics has gotten out of control to the point where we can't disagree on non-salvific issues and remain friendly with another brother or sister in Christ. And most often, the kind of hateful dialogue that is common in our age happens *online*. Many have given up trying to do it face-to-face, and this can be disastrous for a church.

---

1. https://research.lifeway.com/2023/03/07/research-reveals-importance-of-small-groups-evangelism-assimilation-for-church-growth/

2. https://www.pewresearch.org/internet/2023/06/21/as-ai-spreads-experts-predict-the-best-and-worst-changes-in-digital-life-by-2035/

But there are also biblical reasons to press into these smaller communities. Take a close look at Colossians 3:12-16:

> Put on then, as God's chosen ones, holy and beloved, compassionate hearts, kindness, humility, meekness, and patience, bearing with one another and, if one has a complaint against another, forgiving each other; as the Lord has forgiven you, so you also must forgive. And above all these put on love, which binds everything together in perfect harmony. And let the peace of Christ rule in your hearts, to which indeed you were called in one body. And be thankful. Let the word of Christ dwell in you richly, teaching and admonishing one another in all wisdom, singing psalms and hymns and spiritual songs, with thankfulness in your hearts to God.

Paul writes these words to the church in Colossi, *assuming* their connection will include deep love and affection, which requires vulnerability, but it will also include hurt, which requires forgiveness, and it will include worship, teaching, and admonishing. All of this requires significant time together. In our current culture, it is going to be very difficult to get to know everyone in our local church on this kind of deeper level. But that doesn't mean that we shouldn't figure out ways to carry out this exhortation within a church body, which is why we develop smaller groups in a local community that will help us to become more Christlike, and as we do this, we learn to love one another in the way God intends for us to. And when this happens, it serves the larger church body. What makes a web sturdy are all the inner ties woven throughout.

There is something very key here. Being a part of a smaller group of believers is not ultimately about us and what we will get out of it. We are so predisposed to involving ourselves in things that serve *us*, but friends, that is not the way the Bible presents Christian community. In God's beautiful plan for His church, we often experience the reciprocation of love, but we shouldn't join a small group merely to be served; rather, we join a group of believers to love another and aid in their spiritual growth. If we all had this mindset, many churches today would look very different, and, dare I say, function in a much healthier way.

The Benefits and Practicalities of Small Group Ministry

When my mother was dying of a rare brain disease at just sixty years old, I became her primary caretaker. These three years were some of the most trying in my life thus far. Her rapid decline required her to be moved into a care facility, and the disease quickly ripped her of every ability. Her speech was the first function mom lost, so she communicated through screams and groans, and sometimes, quiet crying. There were days when I did not know how to put one foot in front of the other in my care for her.

During this difficult season, I was a part of a small group of women in my church who gathered weekly after Bible study to pray for one another. This small group became not just a balm during these years, but they were a necessity. They pushed me toward Jesus when my bitterness tempted me to pull away, they provided tangibly with meals and childcare, they encouraged me daily through notes, texts, and phone calls, and they cried with me regularly. It was nothing but a joy to reciprocate the love shown to me when I found myself in a season of restoration a few years later. One of the women who had walked this difficult journey with me, about ninety years old at the time, asked me to come and sit with her during her last days on earth. When I think of the reasons to invest in a smaller group of believers, I think of this group of women and the profound ways the Lord used them to teach me about His love.

Experiencing God's love through brothers and sisters is one of the most profound blessings of being a part of a small group of people who know you, and who understand and empathize with your needs. Sometimes these are formal small groups set up by a church, other times they are Sunday School classes or prayer groups that, over time, develop a tight bond. The small group my husband and I were involved with a few years back met during a weeknight, and almost every week I had to push myself to go. I was just worn out by the end of the day, and the idea of pressing on into the evening often felt daunting. But I'll tell you this, I never once regretted going. Being recharged by a small group of fellow believers is not just a balm … it's a necessity, and we sense it when we're with our brothers and our sisters in Christ.

These times together will be most beneficial when we enter them with a biblical framework and an outward focus. Look back at the verse in Colossians. You will reap blessing upon blessing if you go ready and willing to *bear with one another.* According to these verses, Paul means by this that our mindset should be one that is prepared to forgive readily and pour out love unreservedly. It changes the dynamic when we enter a group with a selfless attitude, ready to pour into one another, rather than when we invest with a me-centric attitude. I remember singing the doxology with our small group one night, and as I looked around the room, my eyes filled with tears of gratitude. These folks, whom I wouldn't otherwise know outside of my church community, love Jesus and they love me. It's that realization, as Paul mentions in Colossians, that causes deep thankfulness to God. Your commitment to one another, your vulnerability with others, and your growth in love for one another will all have temporal and eternal benefits.

16

Involvement in Bible Studies

Every Christian should be studying the Scriptures, and if possible, doing so with other believers. I'm certain some will balk at this statement, and, of course, there are seasons in which doing a group Bible study is just not doable. But if it is possible, there are fewer places that you will find deep connectedness than when you are studying the Bible with other believers in your local church.

But isn't my personal time in the Word enough? Yes. The time you carve out for you and your Savior is sufficient. It is necessary. And it is *good*. Be deliberate to set aside time to spend with Jesus, and don't let excuses become your crutch. There are always excuses to not be in the Word, and two of the most common I hear are: I don't have time, and I just can't find quiet time! Friends, what God can do with our limited time is miraculous ... always. You don't need an hour to have effective time with Jesus. And you also don't need quiet. Who came up with the phrase "quiet time," anyway? Your kids might be playing on the floor in front of you, you might hear the clamoring of teenage music, or your coworkers could be bustling around your desk. None of it entirely hinders our ability to open our Bible; in fact, it's a tremendous testimony to family and friends when they see you making the study of Scripture a priority. The Bible is the primary means by which God teaches us who He is. It's the primary means by which He uses the Holy Spirit to direct, guide, convict, and teach us. We *must know our Bibles to know more about Jesus,* so we simply cannot neglect our study of His Word.

So, is a group necessary to study the Bible? No. But it is so helpful to add to your personal time with Jesus. Think of it like an echo chamber. You hear God in your personal time with Him, and then the sounds of His promises, goodness, and His love continue to be echoed throughout your daily existence as you press into other venues of time in God's Word. Deuteronomy 30:14 says, "But the word is very near you. It is in your mouth and in your heart, so that you can do it." Moses says these words to the Israelites before they enter the Promised Land. It's a necessary reminder of the importance of knowing your Bible. It should be so much a part of your life that you cannot help but repeat what it says to others. The repetition of coming back to the Bible time and time again will cause you to hide God's Word in your heart so that when you face hardship or seasons of suffering, His promises surface, providing hope and bringing comfort.

But look at the last part of the verse in Deuteronomy – "so that you can do it." There is a *reason* the Israelites needed to know the Word – so that they could do what it says! The same is true for us; we can't use it to defend our beliefs or to obey what it says if we don't know it. No one can follow the Bible perfectly, and God knows that. But we must try, by the power of His Spirit, to be obedient to what He commands, and obedience to what He commands becomes something we *want* to do when we know and understand our Savior in a deeper way by studying His redemptive story. The more we study it, the more God's Word becomes necessary to us. It takes time and discipline, but eventually you notice that you may even become hungry for it. As the Prophet Ezekiel says in his vision, when he ate the scroll – the words of God – it became in his mouth as sweet as honey (Ezek. 3:3). He wanted more and more.

In college I was invited to join a group Bible study. I had been in discipleship groups in high school but had not yet been a part of a group that was formed for the purpose of studying Scripture together. And to be honest, I had no interest. I was ready with every excuse to not join - it was a bad time of day for me, my schedule was full, I didn't know others in the group, and I preferred playing intramural basketball in my free time (I kept that last excuse to myself). So, I simply said, "No thank you."

I felt convicted while sitting in a class on Shakespeare. Our conversation in class was fascinating, but what made the intricacies of his plays come to life was our lively discussion. I read the same play that my college friends did, but his insights and her perceptions put an exclamation point on what I learned reading it by myself the night before. I considered that if studying classic literature with a group was this amazing, perhaps, if I truly believed what I said I did about Jesus, then studying His Word with others could also be beneficial.

That was over twenty-five years ago, and God has graciously given me the privilege of being a part of different Bible study groups in the churches we've attended through the years. I know there are skeptics who wonder about the significance of a group study, but there is little else that will cause you to feel more connected to others in the church than studying the Word with them. Here are three other benefits to connecting into your local church through a Bible study:

Studying Scripture Together Brings the Bible to Life

Sometimes it's hard to motivate ourselves to open our Bibles. If we are honest, there are times in which we might have felt it to be *boring*. Understand, this is a result of the fall. Our emotions are distorted because we live in a broken world, and because of sin, we easily lose interest in the Scriptures. To be blunt, studying the Bible *is not boring*. There is no book – no matter how well written or long standing – that holds the divine power to change lives like the Bible does. Not one. The Bible puts on display the absolute and perfect glory of God. Its words are divinely inspired, and from the first page of Genesis to the last page in Revelation, God's story unfolds in such a way that causes spontaneous praise, welcome comfort, and energizing joy. We're human, and we need divine intervention to keep our hearts motivated to know God through His Word, and often Jesus will use insights from teachers and other believers to show us the magnificence of His redemptive story.

I have learned so much about the Bible gleaning from the wisdom of Bible study leaders who have studied passages in depth. Their insights into details that I missed awakens my spirit and leaves me excited to learn more. And I have learned much from other sisters whose eyes are opened to a connection between the Old Testament and the New. Their insights enliven my personal study, and, as a result, my love for Jesus.

Studying Scripture Together Provides Clarity

If you struggle with the Bible being too difficult to understand, then one of the best places to be is a small group Bible study. Yes, studying can be hard. But the truths in the Bible are *only found in the Bible.* Studying books about the Bible can be helpful, but they can't replace the spiritual benefits from our study of it.

In a Bible study, one of the goals is to work through some of the more difficult passages together – to learn from each other, to learn from another's gleaning, and to learn from what the leader has studied. I can't tell you how joyful it is to wrestle together through a challenging verse, and then realize how a passage that was once "Greek to me" (well, literally) enhances my understanding of Jesus.

Studying Scripture Together Strengthens the Connection in a Church Body

There's no doubt that it can be intimidating to step into a group study when you don't know the others well. But we are meant to live in community, *and not only amongst people who are just like us* (Rom. 12). Pray before you go. Pray that the Lord will calm your nerves and open your heart to relationships that may not be your "norm," and watch how the Lord provides.

Some of the most precious relationships in my life have stemmed from Bible study groups, but it took investing and committing over time to get to that point. Not every church offers Bible studies, and if that's the case, don't be afraid to start one yourself. Many feel as though doing such a thing should be left to the theologians, but the reality is, every Christian is a theologian. I don't want to take away from the academics who study theology and use their gleanings to teach us about the Bible in depth, but every lay leader can and should study theology without fear. If your faith in God shapes your worldviews, then in this sense, you are a theologian. There is a wealth of resources on how to teach theology well, all of which serve and benefit those who desire to teach the Bible to others.

As you learn with others and grow deeper in your understanding of God and His Word, this growth will serve the larger church community. When your eyes are opened to new understandings in Scripture, or when your faith is refreshed because you've learned something new about a story of old, your worship will naturally be enhanced. Weekly corporate worship with one another is strengthened when we are doing in-depth studies together. Beyond this, we are being equipped to better understand how to sharpen, stir, and encourage one another. The miraculous blessing from God is that His love is revealed to you through His Word, renewing you spiritually, and it is poured out into the lives those you encounter.

The grass withers and the flowers fall, but the Word of our Lord stands forever (Is. 40:8).

17

Cultivating a Desire for Church Involvement in Young Children

Children are so important to the vitality of a local church. We will look later at the incredible benefits of serving the children in our church, but first, it's important to consider how and why connectedness in the local church is important not only for us, but for our children.

Author James K.A. Smith talks about life liturgies, or life habits, in his book, *You Are What You Love*. He says this about the power of spiritual practices: "'Learning' virtue – becoming virtuous – is more like practicing scales on the piano than learning music theory: the goal is, in a sense, for your fingers to learn the scales so they can then play 'naturally', as it were. Learning here isn't just information acquisition; it's more like inscribing something into the very fiber of your being." If your young child has asked why your family attends church outside of Sunday morning, I assure you it won't be the last time they question this life liturgy. As we've already discussed, this is a question every person must wrestle with at some point or another – *why am I doing this church thing?* What we are doing for our young children when we prioritize the local church, is instilling in them patterns that, Lord willing, will be inscribed into the very fiber of their being, so that when they grow into adulthood, they will continue in the spiritual habits that have already become a part of their daily existence.

For a young child, cultivating church involvement begins with the life liturgies you set as their parent. What "rituals" are intertwined in your child's week? If the pattern is that church is only set aside for Sunday mornings, or occasional Sunday mornings, then how can we expect to pass on a desire for our children to connect into the body of Christ? We must teach our children that church is good and necessary not only through our words but through our example.

I remember singing the great hymn *Great is Thy Faithfulness* with a small group of believers after a brief outdoor ceremony. Holding my youngest in my arms, she whispered in my ear, *"How do you know the words, momma?"* For a moment, I thought back to my own childhood in the pews of my church, listening to the hymns as I colored on my bulletin. I pictured my grandfather singing the hymn boisterously during family vacations. I pictured my dad singing it from the stage on a Sunday morning, and I saw, in my mind's eye, my mom singing the words over my father's death bed. *"Great is thy faithfulness, O God my Father. There is no shadow of turning with Thee..."* No one made me memorize it; no one sat down to teach it to me. I learned it by listening, observing, and putting into practice what I learned through the years. The rote singing of that hymn eventually became instilled words that acted as a balm throughout many challenging seasons in my life. Parent, when you involve yourself in the church, when you love Christ's bride so much that being a part of her ministries is something you *desire,* you are setting an example for your children. They are listening and observing, and Lord willing, one day church involvement will become an integral part of their own life. And rest assured that this connectedness in a local church will become more and more important as our secular culture is increasingly vying for our children's attention and seeking to mold their beliefs. So, first and foremost, pass on to your young children a desire to be involved in a local church community by making church connectedness a life liturgy for you and your family.

And there are usually varying ministries in a church for children to connect into. It's easy to think of ministries like Sunday school or a midweek kid's ministry night as simply childcare. But beyond what they are hopefully learning about God and His Word during these times, children are getting to know other kids in the church. The relationships they build at church when they are young will be an important part of their staying connected during the teen years, but it's difficult for our kids to get to know others if their involvement is limited to sitting in a worship service on Sundays.

In addition, involvement in varying ministries outside of Sunday morning worship will connect your children to adults, many of whom will love them and may be an integral part of their growth in Jesus. Some of the Sunday school teachers I had as a child were formative in my spiritual walk, and they taught me lessons that I have not soon forgotten. I remember the Books of the Bible song Mrs. Bryce taught me, and I still utter its tune when the pastor tells us to flip over to a particular book; I remember how Mr. Talent patiently answered our many questions as fifth and sixth graders, and I will never forget sitting around the table on a Wednesday night as various adults from the church inquired about my school day. It all made an impact, and it all helped me as a child to feel like I belonged to our church body.

When our kids are young, if their only friendships are outside of church, then getting them to attend other ministries may become a battle. But even with internal friendships, sometimes kids fight going to Sunday church or to a midweek ministry event. This is hard, parents, there's no doubt about it. But it's also quite natural. Haven't there been times when you didn't want to go back out to a Bible study on a Wednesday evening or a choir rehearsal on a Tuesday night? It is most often the case that we are glad we go, but sometimes it's hard to get out the door. It's no different for your children. Empathizing goes a long way, but I would urge you to not get into the practice of skipping each time they resist going. The pattern will only become cyclical. Involving our families in the ministry of the church is a form of discipleship. Their resistance is a good time to instruct and teach them why it's important for your family to be involved: remind them of how important they are to your local church community. Kids need to hear that sometimes their presence encourages another child in attendance or even their own teacher who has prepared a lesson. These kinds of conversations are how we disciple our children in the Lord.

None of this ensures that your child will one day grow to love and involve themselves in a local church community, but it sure might be a part of their testimony as to why they stayed connected. Teach your children through instruction and example what it looks like to love and commit to the church that God loves so much that He gave His very life for her.

18

Cultivating a Desire for Church Involvement in Teens

To be frank, encouraging teens to see the importance of involvement in their local church can be difficult. It's hard enough for adults to determine that involvement is important but cultivating a desire for church involvement in teens whose lives are filled to the brim with activities, whose emotions are, at times, all over the place, and who are figuring out for themselves what they believe, is just plain challenging. But, parents, *it's still important.* The easy thing to do with teens is reduce church to a checklist item that we cross off to make *us* feel better. If they attend Sunday morning, we feel like we've done what we needed to do, and our kid was fed the necessary spirituality to get through the week. Conversely, we can be off balance in the other extreme of expecting too much of our teens when it comes to church involvement. As an adult, you might be able to make it to church for several service and ministry opportunities during a month, but we must be careful about requiring our children to match our involvement. Remember, the church does not save our kids. God does.

So, why then concern ourselves with cultivating in our teens a need to commit and involve themselves in the local church? If we are going to disciple the next generation about the significance of Christ's bride, then we cannot reduce the role of the church to something that provides for them for an hour on Sunday morning. The ones who will carry on the vitality of the next generation of churches are the tweens and teens that you sit next to on a Sunday morning. Statistics show that, out of every ten students in your church, only about three teens will stay involved in the church into college. What can we do about this? First and foremost, we must be daily praying that God would raise up leaders who love and desire to serve the church of Christ, but we must simultaneously be discipling, teaching our teens by word and example why the church should remain central in their life.

As a child, my mom used to reinforce the importance of brushing my teeth morning and evening, *but I hated doing it.* If she felt like instruction was enough, my teeth would have rotted as a child! She not only told me about the importance of this pattern, but showed me how to do it, and then brought me regularly, sometimes kicking and screaming, to the dentist. Over time, I experienced the consequences of not caring for my teeth, and eventually, I had to decide for myself that if I wanted to maintain a nice smile and not have a large bill from dental work, I was going to need to do something. And so, I put into practice what my mom taught me, and eventually passed on the same instruction to my own kiddos. This is the same kind of learning experience I had with church involvement. If my parents left it at instruction without example and experience, it would have been more difficult for me to see the benefit of church involvement in my own life. But my parents taught me, both through example and instruction, that being a regular part of the local church was important. They did some pushing when necessary and some hand holding (and pulling) when needed, and eventually I decided for myself that this was a healthy and necessary pattern. It started with their teaching, kept on with their urging, and caught on because of the Holy Spirit's work in my life and in my parent's leading. It was my second year in college that I remember looking around my new church congregation, and I thought, *if I'm going to make an impact, I must do something.* And so, I got involved volunteering with the youth group and the church nursery.

There are a myriad of ways our teens can involve themselves in the local church. From serving in a food pantry or cleaning up the bulletins on a Sunday morning, to setting up chairs or joining the music team, teens can involve themselves in the same ways adults can. It's not complicated, and it doesn't have to be taxing for it to be effective both for our teens and for the larger church body. But teens are also in a strange in between space where they are no longer a child, but they are not yet independent adults (although often they would like to think they are). Think of this "in between space" in our churches. Teens are too old for children's ministry, and they are too young for some of the adult classes in the sense that most teenagers are looking for something to relationally connect them – to help them feel like they belong. While they might understand adult small groups or Bible studies, they aren't necessarily going to find the kind of connectedness they long for in these places. This is why many churches offer youth groups.

Youth group is one of the most important ways for a teen to connect themselves into a local church, but in this culture, there is a lot of push back on this. Sports, increased college demands, and the super-busy families that make up our churches, are all causing church youth groups to decrease in size. They just can't compete with everything that a teen today has going on. Is youth group, then, even worth it? Isn't it just a modern idea that is now outdated? I don't think so. Many of Jesus' disciples were not older men when He first called them. In fact, some theologians believe that at least a few of the disciples may have been in their teens when they began following Jesus. In Matthew 17:24-27, Jesus pays the Temple tax for Himself and for Peter. It's likely this was the case because they were the only ones in the group over the age accountable to pay the tax (at twenty years old). We don't know exactly the age of the disciples, but the point is, a few of them were likely teens who were invested in and then sent off to do the work of the kingdom. In this, Jesus sets an example for us when it comes to the importance of discipling the next generation of the church. Of course, parents play the primary role when it comes to discipleship, but we were never meant to be alone in the task. Even in the early church days, while the primary job of raising children fell to the parent, many of them lived amongst and with others from their church body, so they would contribute together to the tasks of discipleship.

All of this lays the groundwork for youth ministry in churches. All over the world, the Lord is using these youth ministries to connect teens into their local churches and to draw young people to Himself. When our new members stand and give a brief testimony at our church, often, we hear that a person came to know the Lord either through the children's ministry at their church or through the discipleship of a leader in their youth group. God works in these ministries, and they not are not just a place for a teen to grab pizza and play silly games. They are an important part of the vitality of the church, and through them, your teen can be spiritually impacted in deep and significant ways.

While a youth ministry can - and should - effectively help to connect your teen into the larger body of the church, there are certainly unhealthy extremes between the church and the church's youth group. If a group is only served but never serves, it loses its effectiveness at connecting youth into the body of believers. A youth group should not be its own island in a local church. This does not ultimately serve the teens or the larger church body. It's difficult for teens to transition into adult ministry if their youth group held separate worship services and separate everything else from the larger body of believers. That's not a healthy model for connectedness, and teens who experience this do not integrate well into adult ministry after graduation. On the other hand, the youth group can too easily be utilized as the ones to call on for *all the things* when ministry leaders can't find sufficient volunteers. While youth should be serving in the larger church body, there is something unique about the relationships formed and the discipleship that happens when the youth kids have their own time together.

So, what if your teen wants to go to a different youth group than the one your church provides? It's a great question, and one that is asked often. It's also one my own father was confronted with when my sister asked to attend another church's youth group. Don't shut it down right away, but have a conversation with your teen about it, and find out why it is that they want to attend elsewhere. Sometimes, and really most of the time, its social reasons, but not always. Find out why they're asking. And then assess the spiritual maturity of your child. If your teen is showing a new interest in church that you've been praying God would put on their heart, then keeping them from more exposure to God's Word – even at a different church – is usually counter-productive. By all means, encourage the interest!

On the other hand, if you notice some spiritual maturity in your teen, then talk with them about the importance of committing first and foremost to the church that God has called your family to commit to. Skipping this step, whether intentionally or not, teaches our children that commitment is only important when it serves us and our needs. This is not how God intended for His church to function. We don't want to create a generation of church hoppers that pick and choose where they go based on what serves them. Prayerfully consider your answer. It might be that you that you ask your teen to commit to your youth group to keep their covenant with Christ's body by being a faithful member of this group, and if they're willing to do that, then they can attend other events or meetings at another youth group in addition to their own.

If you desire that your teen be a part of the youth ministry at your church, but you find that they are regularly resisting it altogether, here are a few possible responses to consider.[1]

Listen

Listening intently is important and shows your teens that you acknowledge their perspective. Is it that they don't have many close friends who attend? Are they having trouble connecting with a particular leader? Or are they perhaps struggling with doubt, causing them to withdraw a bit?

Perhaps there are some good reasons for your teen to avoid attendance. In that case, it's important to seek solutions. Rather than jumping in to fix things for them, listening gives us an opportunity to help them wrestle through the issues and guide them in problem-solving. The solution may be something as simple as meeting with a youth minister to lovingly share concerns and attentively listen to his or her insights. Listening shouldn't result in passivity but in activity, and by God's grace, it may even lead to a conversation that draws you closer to each other.

Pray for these conversations and ask the Lord to open the door for a good, healthy discussion and an abundance of wisdom to know how to respond. And saturate the youth ministries in your church with prayer. If you believe church ministry to our teens is valuable and that their involvement is important, then it's certainly worth the time to listen and discuss ways to overcome some of the hurdles that are keeping them from attending.

Exhort

Sometimes listening should lead to exhortation – communicating with encouragement and strong urging. There are a couple reasons to exhort our kids to attend youth group.

---

1. The following was originally published on Rooted Ministry: *https://rootedministry.com/three-responses-to-a-teenager-resisting-youth-group/)*

First and foremost, youth ministry within the local church exposes our kids to the gospel. As Christian parents, we want our children to have as much exposure as possible to the good news that Jesus came to earth, died for our sins, and rose again. This is the hope we all need to be reminded of daily. Youth group meetings outside of regular Sunday morning worship reinforce gospel truths so that, by God's grace, our kids will begin to know, grasp, and understand God's love for them. We exhort our teenagers to attend out of a desire to see them grow spiritually.

Involvement in youth ministry also teaches our kids what it means to have the church be a part of their daily liturgies. The body of Christ is a precious gift, and the Lord cares about our involvement in it (Heb. 10:25). Many of the patterns our teens set now will follow them into adulthood, and our hope is that connection to the Body of Christ will not be merely one of many activities to choose from, but a necessary part of their daily routines.

Lastly, the exhortation to attend comes from having a broader perspective on what a teenager's attendance means for the body. Your teenager may not have considered that his participation is not just about him, but an encouragement to the body of Christ. Youth leaders put time and energy into lessons, games, and preparations, so your teen's presence is a way of showing love and respect for the care provided. Other students need your teen's presence. We all know that in junior high and high school, numbers encourage numbers. The urging to attend is for the sake of the group as a whole – each teenager is an important part of a larger body of believers.

Exemplify

One of the greatest temptations we fall into is having a consumer mentality when it comes to our churches. There is no perfect church, so it's easy to find things to complain about. The most important thing is that our churches are faithfully teaching the Scriptures and leading God's people in spirit and in truth (2 Tim. 4:3). If you've made a commitment to a church because you believe in its mission and ministry, then the primary question should be: "What can I give?" rather than, "What can I get?"

We are called to live this out as parents, setting the example by seeking ways to involve ourselves in ministries that will be encouraged by our presence. It's important to consider our own level of commitment not only for our spiritual vitality, but for the sake of setting an example for our teens. Ask Jesus to open your eyes to the places you can involve yourself even now to strengthen your relationship both with God and with His people. You are an important part of a larger body of believers.

Be encouraged, parent. God is at work in our teenagers' hearts—even in the midst of our inconsistencies. God is so good, and He loves our kids more than we ever could. Even in their resistance, you can point them to His faithful love, which we pray will draw their hearts to know Jesus more.

Pray for the teens in your church. Pray that God might work in them now to make an impact in the next generation of the church. Pray for the young children who are learning who Jesus is and what His word says. Pray for your own involvement in your church, that you might be open to where God is calling you to plug in and get connected. And pray for the ministries that are ongoing that Satan might be bound from his destruction and that they might be used to strengthen the church body and proclaim the gospel of Jesus Christ.

PART FOUR:
Loving God's People:
The Importance of Embracing
Our Church Family

And let us consider how to stir up one another to love and good works, not neglecting to meet together, as is the habit of some, but encouraging one another, and all the more as you see the Day drawing near.

Hebrews 10:24-25

19

On Vulnerability with Church Community

My husband and I trudged into church emotionally and physically exhausted. Neither of us slept the night before due to a challenging evening with one of our teens. But duty called – my husband was scheduled to preach, and I was leading worship. There before anyone else, I stood at the front of the sanctuary and looked at the empty chairs which would soon be filled with people who know me. *But do they?* I stood contemplating. *Do these people really know me? Do they have any hint of my soul-wounds or my deep anxiety, and should they?* Spiritual fatigue seeped in as I wondered how I would put on my "together" face. I tried on an awkward smile, but tears combatted my attempt, and I relented to them. *Close up the pain,* I thought, *seal it up until the service is finished and the doors of the church are shut.*

I know I'm not alone with these kinds of emotions because I've heard them uttered, and I've read them expressed. There's tension for the congregant who feels they must hide their sincere emotion and enter the sanctuary by accepting the smiling mask and then returning it when they leave.

The exhortation to love one another is prominent in the New Testament, but the question is, *can we love without being vulnerable with one another*? Of course, the phrase "being vulnerable" is one that is embraced by some and scoffed at by others. One might see vulnerability as an unnecessary spewing of emotion, while the other sees it as a necessary risk to achieve real love and connectedness. Like most changes in generations, the pendulum swings hard from one side to the other, and it seems there is a reaction to the perceived stoicism of many in the older generation of the church. As a result, those younger are desiring intimacy but are having a hard time finding what they deem people being "real" within the church's walls.

There are many reasons for this, some of which stem from churches that rarely incorporate lament in their worship. To lament sin, and to sing honest songs that cry out to God, requires a certain vulnerability on our part, but churches don't always readily incorporate these emotions in worship. Some would rather keep the service upbeat and uplifting. But our worship should ebb and flow in emotion, much like the Psalms do, and in doing so, a church will begin to create an atmosphere of honesty before God, and in turn, before others.

But vulnerability can also be misunderstood. We've bought into the world's definition that opening up, or being vulnerable, is for the purpose of self-fulfillment. Tainted by sin, vulnerability can be incredibly self-serving and sometimes manipulative. But there is a redemptive form of vulnerability that is not self-seeking and can be used as an avenue to better love others in our midst. We see this in the New Testament with the many "one another" exhortations. Loving one another is embodied in the actions of praying for one another (Eph. 6:18), bearing one another's burdens (Gal. 6:2), confessing to one another (James 5:16), and forgiving each another (Eph. 4:31-32). None of these can happen without some willingness to honestly bare your soul, even with just a few.

What this doesn't mean is that every person in our church needs full access to the bottle of emotions that we carry around, nor does it mean that we must share our deepest concerns with every person we meet. That is the "emotional spewing" that is off-putting to some, and it's not always helpful toward strengthening the body. There is certainly wisdom in knowing what to share and with whom to share it. But when *no one* in the church knows your scars, your fears, or your hurts, we cannot affectively love you in the way we're called to love. The younger generation's plea for vulnerability is a reaction to an unwillingness of some to share personally and honestly. Jesus set the ultimate example of vulnerability when He took on the weakness of human flesh for you and for me: "...Though he was in the form of God, did not count equality with God a thing to be grasped, but emptied himself, by taking the form of a servant, being born in the likeness of men" (Phil. 2).

But vulnerability is not without risk. There is, at times, a cost when you open up to some in your church. C.S. Lewis in his book *The Four Loves* says this about the risky aspect of love and vulnerability: "There is no safe investment. To love at all is to be vulnerable. Love anything, and your heart will certainly be wrung and possibly broken. If you want to make sure of keeping it intact, you must give your heart to no one, not even to an animal. Wrap it carefully round with hobbies and little luxuries; avoid all entanglements; lock it up safe in the casket or coffin of your selfishness."[1] Sometimes we will get hurt by the people we open up to. That is part of our fallen human nature and a reality of living in a broken world. My pastor-father used to talk about the people in his congregation as sheep that he shepherded. He loved the people he cared for, "But," he'd say, "sheep have teeth, and they sure can bite."

Not only is it risky, but vulnerability can be emotionally taxing if we are seeing it in a redemptive way. You see, sometimes people want to be known and heard, but they do not want to reciprocate. They view their pain as ultimate and roll their eyes inwardly at anyone else's hardships. But redemptive vulnerability sees the openness as a give-and-take because it is ultimately *for the betterment of the body of Christ.* Sometimes

---

1. Lewis, C. S., *The Four Loves* (London: Harcourt, 1960), as quoted in: Zach Kincaid, "Four Types of Love" C. S. Lewis, Feb 13, 2020, cslewis.com/four-types-of-love/#:~:text=There%20is%20no%20safe%20investment,perturbations%20of%20love%20is%20Hell. Last accessed Nov 4, 2024.

loving another means sitting with them in the trenches of their pain and hurt, even when we're carrying our own burdens. To love in the selfless way Christ exemplified might mean walking with someone in their pain, no matter how messy that might be.

Redemptive vulnerability comes with an understanding that our ultimate identity is *in Christ*. When we start there, we have the solid and secure promise that we are already accepted and loved unconditionally which takes away the temptation to manipulate others with our emotions to gain more love through attention. Jesus cannot love you more than He already does. And that truth also frees us to put away the mask we feel we must wear on Sundays in fear that people will be put off by our failures and insecurities. I think of the apostle Paul who demonstrated this when he wrote to the Corinthians: "Be imitators of me, as I am of Christ" (1 Cor. 11:1). In other words, Paul tells the church in Corinth to imitate Christ in him who is working in and through Paul's weaknesses. The subtle messages that social media sends of the "perfect" family causes us to believe that to be accepted is to put on that "have it all together" façade. And yet, Paul says, *I boast in my weakness* (2 Cor. 12:9) because it is in our inabilities that Christ's glory is made known. If you struggle to open up to anyone, you are missing the opportunity to point another to Christ by exemplifying the reality that where you are weak, He is strong. Where you are unable, Christ is fully able. To be a disciple maker, we must tell this message about Christ through our own vulnerability.

That Sunday morning when I came to church wearied and burdened, I could not hold in my emotion, and I believe that was a gift from the Lord. The first person I encountered was a woman in the hallway who asked how I was doing and probably was not prepared for the response she received. This dear woman caught the emotions that poured out of my pent-up bottle and added to them her own empathetic tears. There were no easy answers or immediate solutions, but I felt known, and I was prayed over as she helped me carry my burdens to the foot of the cross. Even years later, this congregant follows up and prays regularly for my children.

Do you have an intimate group of Christ followers where redemptive vulnerability is present? Do you set the example, or are you waiting for someone else to take the lead while slowly becoming embittered by impatiently wearing your mask? Take a risk – love others in the way that Christ has called us to love for the sake of the church and the gospel of Christ.

20

Loving God's People When You've Been Hurt by the Church

The title of the post immediately caught my eye: "*Why I Quit the Church.*" The author went into the way in which he had been hurt by the church, so he decided to simply walk away from it altogether. "I still love Jesus," he claimed, "but I no longer love the church." His hurt was palpable, and much of it I empathized with.

Church Hurt is Real

I've trudged through my own church hurt journeys through the years. As a teen, I remember snide comments about my pastor-father when he sought to plant a new church and build a building necessarily larger than the one he was currently pastoring in. "The king wants a bigger castle," was one comment that left an imprint. *Why did congregants jump to assuming my father was seeking this plant by himself and for himself?* But many did, and their accusations hurt.

I watched my mother walk through a very difficult church split after my father passed away. When she told me about some of the hard statements made at a congregational meeting, my heart broke as she described her hurt. And in one difficult season of our ministry, my husband and I felt betrayed by a church leader and his wife whom we considered good friends. After serving alongside us for several years, they sent a note informing us they would no longer be attending the church. There was no explanation and no expounding other than,

"We think another couple would be a better fit as our pastor and pastor's wife. God bless." We tried to reach out, but they would not respond, so we never spoke again. I still feel the hurt surface when I return to that memory.

In writing these things, I'm not suggesting that those involved were 100 per cent in the wrong, but rather to underline how painful and difficult church conflict can be for everyone. I know that some have been hurt by the church in ways far deeper than these examples. I've lamented with friends who bear the scars from this kind of hurt, and it's painful. If you have experienced church hurt, I'm deeply sorry for the grief that has caused. *El Roi,* the God Who Sees, looks not dismissively, but in the same way He saw Hagar and provided comfort in her despair (Gen. 16), God sees you. Your story is not invisible to Him, so there is no need to defend the hurt because you can rest assured that God sees it and knows it. He is tender and compassionate, and He is just. There will be a day when justice will roll down like mighty water, and all that has been wronged will be made right by the hand of God who created all things.

Why We Cannot Quit the Church

I share just a snippet of personal stories not to compare pain, but to say that I understand some form of church hurt and the hurt that ripples in its wake. There has been grave damage done to congregants by churches through the years, especially by local churches who seem to care more about power and self-protection than the people in their care. And yet, as believers in Jesus, we cannot quit the church altogether. As much as the pain is undeniable, so is God's truth in Scripture, and He makes clear that the church is precious to Him. We cannot use hurt as an excuse to divorce ourselves from this institution. We cannot quit the church; *we are the church.* What kind of friend would I be to Jesus if I didn't also strive to love and serve His bride? Theologian and author Michael Horton once said, "*The visible church is where you will find Christ's kingdom on earth, and to disregard the kingdom is to disregard its King.*"[1]

Christ loves His church, so we can't resolve to hate it, nor can we be OK to simply leave it all together. Ephesians 5:25 says that "Christ loved the church and gave himself up for her." Do you see the profound love? Believers, this not my personal conviction, but it is God's words. All of us - congregants and leaders alike – are sinners, so we should not be surprised that we fail to love the church like Christ does. But understand that when you allow your hurt to turn into hatred toward the institution of the church, you're doing damage to your faith, to the witness of the gospel, and you are turning your back on what God says He loves enough to give His life for.

Church Realities

It has been said a few times, but it's worth emphasizing again – do not attempt to find a church that you believe does not make mistakes. You will eventually be sorely disappointed because the church is made up of people, and people can, and usually will, hurt you in some form or another. The sin may be something as small as an insensitive comment by a congregant or as hurtful as the moral failure of a pastor. When a leader falls, trust is broken, and that's an incredibly painful experience. We put our trust in our church leaders as ones who are called to spiritually equip and lead our families, so the fracture their sins can cause, even sometimes leading to church splits, is not surprising, though it is deeply sad and disruptive to the gospel witness. It is equally disheartening when believers act in ways that are so ungodly that it makes you question what the Bible says. When there is no accountability for the leadership, these kinds of situations are increasingly common and profoundly damaging to the church's witness in our world.

---

1. Forward by Michael Horton taken from *Church Membership* by Jonathan Leeman, (Wheaton, IL: Crossway Books, 2012), p. 15.

This is exactly why we should never join a church merely because of a leader we like. Leaders will come and go, and leaders may fail you. But God will never break His promises, He will never betray you or turn His back on you, and He does not do that to His church when it faces tumult and turmoil in this life. There is consequence to sin, and our God does not turn a blind eye to disobedience, but neither does He walk away from His bride altogether.

Interestingly, church hurt is not a new concept in our modern world. The Bible itself is full of examples of church hurt all the way back to the Old Testament when Hannah is mistreated by Eli the Priest (1 Sam. 1:4-20), to the New Testament where Paul is neglected by the church in Rome (2 Tim. 4:10, 16). Church hurt is not new, because sin is not new. In fact, if you think about it, most of the New Testament is written to churches because they are facing issues in some form or another. Almost all of Paul's letters are written to help an erring church from getting too far off track.

I remember one dear young man who was nominated for elder in one of our churches. He was qualified in every biblical way, but I told my husband I was nervous about him stepping into this role only because the deeper you go into church life, the more the curtains are pulled back and you tend to see, more clearly, the sin that touches every aspect of God's church. This sin can be disheartening, and yet, investing deeply in the life of the church can also be profoundly beautiful.

Friends, Satan *hates* the church, and what he desires is to see it's work thwarted in any way possible. He does a tremendous job getting in the middle of relationships, causing us to unnecessarily distrust leaders. He distracts us in worship with nonsensical things like the outfit someone is wearing. Satan will do anything to get our eyes off the gospel of Jesus Christ. But what is amazing is seeing the up-close ways that God does His work *despite Satan's attempts to disrupt it.* Although many institutions and kingdoms have fallen through the centuries, that will not happen to the church of God. It's miraculous, and yet, it's not surprising. It's God's ordained institution; the church is His beloved bride. He is not going to let Satan have his ultimate way. He may win some church battles in this life, but Jesus gave Himself up for the church and will continue to fight for her until the day He returns. The gates of hell will not prevail against the church because Christ is already the victor.

A Way Forward

There is no doubt that healing is necessary to keep loving God's people in these painful situations. Confront the hurt. Be willing to grieve it and understand it, but know that, as you process your pain, there is always a way forward. Sometimes healing happens when you keep plodding through the mess because the reality is, another mess will likely come. Of course, there are some places or situations that are unsafe, and there are times to disengage and find a new church home, but as is the case with most relationships that have been through rocky times, when you come out on the other side with healing and forgiveness, you are stronger together than you were before.

And don't neglect prayer and meditation on God's Word. Pray regularly and first and foremost for your own heart. Pray that the Lord will soften your heart toward those who have hurt you. Bitterness towards another spreads far and fast, and it can be one of the greatest hinderances to our spiritual growth. Pray also that God will provide the discernment necessary to know how to process the pain. His Word is truth, and it speaks to all circumstances we face in this life, so open it and mediate on it, and through it, trust that God will provide the wisdom necessary to know how to navigate church hurt. Don't quit the church, believer. Find a way forward in the strength of Christ and be open to learning what it means to love His bride.

21

Loving God's People Intergenerationally

"Dear Katie,
Thinking and praying for you. When a diamond is found, the jeweler cuts, cuts, and cuts again and again. When the Lord loves a saint so much, he may spare others certain trials, but not this one. You are his beloved. Rejoice in it."

These words were emailed to me about ten years ago from a ninety-year-old saint in our church, named Wanda. It was during the time I mentioned previously, when my mom was terminally ill and failing quickly. She required around-the-clock care, and since my father had passed away, I became mom's primary caretaker. My children were still young at the time, so I often felt pulled at the seams, as though at any moment my life might unravel. While I had very little time to myself, for two hours each week, I attended a women's Bible study and the prayer group that followed. As I think back on that time, I remember this break in my week as a balm to my soul. I was so weary, physically and emotionally, but those two hours refueled me in unique and unexpected ways.

My prayer group was made up of women who were mostly older than me, including dear "Miss Wanda." The day before receiving the email, I lamented with my prayer group that I felt disoriented from what seemed like God's angry hand on my life. Wanda's encouraging and mother-like exhortation reminded me that the Lord was not against me during the trial, but He was for me, and, perhaps most importantly, *He was working in me.* That email meant so much to me that I printed it out and still have it in my Bible. Week after week Wanda checked in, asked me how she could pray, and then offered a word of encouragement. Though she was physically weaker merely due to age, the Lord used her to hold me up and carry me through some of the toughest days in my life thus far.

When mom passed away, Miss Wanda stepped in as a surrogate grandma and had a sweet relationship with my youngest who shared Miss Wanda's love for gardening. When Wanda gardened around our church, she always called my Lily to come and help her, and Lily never went begrudgingly, but always with great excitement. While my daughter was somewhat interested in the kind of flowers they'd be planting, she mostly just enjoyed Miss Wanda's willing ear. Lily talked that ear off, telling Wanda all the things about all the things, and Wanda just smiled when I asked if her if she was able to get any words in.

And then, in the last weeks of Wanda's life, she called for my husband and I to come and sit with her. Emails had been exchanged regarding her desires for the funeral, so we talked through those details, read Scripture, laughed at memories of Lily, and sometimes, we just sat. Miss Wanda died peacefully, and though she has been with her Savior for several years, I still talk of her often, and so does my daughter.

The Blessing of Intergenerational Relationships

One of the greatest gifts in God's church is the opportunity to love intergenerationally. It's quite a different thing to say that your church is "multi-generational" than it is to say that it's "intergenerational." Multi-generation merely means that differing generations are present. Intergenerational implies that they are interacting in some way. In a multi-generational church, it's easy to seek out relationships in the church with only those in the same stage of life, and those kinds of friendships are certainly important. There is something to be said about investing in relationships with those who are "in the trenches" with you, so to speak. And yet, if we limit ourselves to building relationships in the church with only those who are like us or in the same stage of life as us, we miss out on the benefits of intergenerational relationships, including mentorship, necessary perspective, and uniquely effective service. I experienced this with Miss Wanda, but also through numerous other relationships in the church through the years. There is one dear woman, at least fifteen years younger, who has shared some of the most profound wisdom with me; while I often see myself as a mentor, the reciprocity in the relationship is one of God's greatest blessings. When you give, you will receive (Luke 6:38). God tells us this will happen, but we're sometimes skeptical, because we often only understand "receiving" through a very narrow lens.

How Intergenerational Relationships are Formed

Sometimes these intergenerational relationships in the church happen naturally, through a small group or Bible study, but often, churches will form their ministries around people in the same age or stage of life. Think through the last couple of small groups or ministries you have connected into. Have they been made up of people varying in ages, or was everyone in the same season of life? And was there cultural and ethnic diversity represented? You see, it's easy, and sometimes less messy, to get involved in church communities with people who are like us and who walk a similar path to us. But to seclude yourself in this way robs you of the immense blessing of learning from someone older, of pouring into someone younger, and of gleaning important wisdom from a person who has differing perspectives that you may not have considered.

I remember reading a social media post one time from a person who was looking to find deeper friendships within their church. They went on to list several "qualifications" for potential friends which included being in the same stage of life, aligning with this person's views on politics, and living nearby. Friends, this way of thinking when pursuing relationships in the church misses such a huge part of what God intended when He exhorts us in the New Testament to *love one another.* He didn't intend for that exhortation to apply only to those who are like us as though there are caveats to His command. Jesus gives us a glimpse of this in Revelation through John's vision of the church universal which is unified as one body and people from every tribe and language and people and nation all singing praises to God together (Rev. 5:9). Our churches should be foretastes of what is to come! This means seeking out ways that you can build relationships in your local church with those who are not necessarily like you, including those in differing stages and places in life. It means actively pursuing mentorship and discipleship, which Jesus Himself modeled for us during His life on earth.

If we think we can't gain wisdom from someone who may think a bit differently than us, especially on non-salvific issues, then we've lost sight of what it means to love the people of God in all humility and gentleness (Eph. 4:1). If we don't believe we have anything to learn from someone who is older, then we've let pride take root and have forgotten that the Bible tells us that some of the greatest earthly wisdom comes from the aged (Job 12:12). And if we aren't actively seeking to disciple someone in some form or another, then we're not sharpening each other in the way Jesus modeled for us (Prov. 27:17). These kinds of relationships might occur when planting flowers with a six-year-old, and they might happen when studying Scripture with a ninety-year-old. Either way, you will be blessed, and perhaps even for many years to come.

22

Loving God's People When I'm New to My Church

I can imagine that some might wonder why I wouldn't address the long-time members on how to love those new to the congregation, and not the other way around. To be sure, both have equal significance. Long-time members must be looking for ways to love those who are new to a church, and if the church is too large to know who is new and who is not, take a chance and introduce yourself. Hold out a hand to someone you haven't met and ask them if they're new or if they've been attending for a while. If a church relents to not welcoming people into their midst in the way that Christ has readily welcomed us as His children, then it can quickly feel cold and exclusive. Think of how Christ has received us. It's not based on our outward appearance (1 Sam. 16:7); it's not because of anything we've done for Him (Gal. 2:21); and it's always with love (Eph. 2:4-5). We should have Christ's reception in mind when looking into the eyes of someone in our church body that we don't know, and even more so, when we're looking at someone who may not look just like us. A genuine welcome into the house of God brings glory to God (Rom. 15:7).

Years ago, my husband and I visited a church during a Sunday we had off and had a very interesting experience. The first thing we noticed, glancing around from the back of the sanctuary, was that not one single or couple was over sixty. The congregation was uniform in stage and age of life, most between about twenty and thirty years old. We later found out that the vision of the new church was to be a place for young people. In theory, the idea sounded great, and it was certainly welcoming to many younger folks. But we wondered: what would happen when the youngers grew older? Would they relocate and replenish with new twenties and thirties? Interestingly, nearly twenty years later, that church has reconfigured its mission.

The second thing we noticed was that no one spoke to us. We didn't attend the church that morning to see if this would be the case; rather, we attended to be refreshed by worship as congregants and not leaders. However, we couldn't shake the disconcerted feeling until we both realized how *unwelcomed* we were. Friends, be the person in your church who brings warmth to a cold room. Be the one who extends a hand so that someone might experience the extension of God's tender grace. It goes a long way in someone's church experience, whether they're a believer or not.

What's even harder, I think, is committing to a new church and figuring out what loving God's people looks like when you don't know a soul. But it's important because if this isn't prioritized, you will feel disconnected and be tempted to leave because of it. Remember, God didn't give us caveats on the command to love one another. It's not, "after one year" love one another, or "when you feel comfortable," love one another. The Bible says, "*Love one another just as I have loved you…*" (John 13:34-35). There are no limitations and no stipulations and no exceptions. That means, when you commit to a body of believers, you are committing to get busy loving on people in your midst.

So, what does this look like in a church where I don't really know the people?

Learn Names

First, do your best to learn names. I remember sitting in a meeting one time with several fellow employees. Our boss began the meeting by explaining that we should not expect her to be able to remember our names. Names were hard for her, and so it's better if we just accept that she'll not recall our name and know that it's nothing personal. But it is personal! It's my name. Look, we can't possibly remember everyone's name that we meet when we're new, but we can make a concerted effort to do so rather than being lackadaisical about it. Sometimes it helps to repeat the name, to write it down, or to make a connection that will help you remember the next time you see that person. Make a goal to introduce yourself to one new person each Sunday, and then try to remember their name. Sometimes it helps to pray for that person during the week, even if you don't know them well. Praying for them by name reinforces a natural connectedness. When you're new, *this is hard*. If you're introverted, *this is hard*. If you're self-conscious and can't remember if you already introduced yourself, *this is hard*. But it's better to love another with a welcoming word, and every-so-often make a fool of ourselves, then it is to stay quiet and unwelcoming. Making an effort to learn a few names right away will go a long way in loving another as a newcomer as it says, "I care for you as a sister or brother in Christ."

Offer Hospitality

Second, invite people into your home. And really, this goes for anyone who is feeling disconnected from people at church. I'm the pastor's wife, and there are seasons when I feel disconnected from people in the church for all sorts of varying reasons, but when you have folks into your space, a natural bond begins to strengthen, and that sense of feeling connected starts to return. If this is hard for you, there are multiple resources available on what it looks like to offer hospitality, but I can at least tell you this. My husband and I have been inviting people into our home since our first year of marriage. Some of these people we have known well, and some we had only met with a handshake, but every time we are blessed. *Every time.* I do not recall one evening over dinner that I regret in nearly twenty-five years of ministry. And folks, I don't like to cook, my home is not super spacious nor is it immaculate, and when my kids were little, they were running all around the company. Now our dog has taken the place of their little feet, but with an annoying bark instead of cute, little voices offering hellos. The point is, there will always be excuses and hinderances, but don't let those things stop you from getting to know someone better by having them over to your house.

Get Involved

And lastly, volunteer. Pray that the Lord will clearly direct where you might serve, and then get involved. There is very little that will help you get to know others in the church better than serving alongside of them. This is the first thing I ask about when someone tells me they are having a hard time developing friendships in their new church. Some of my closest friends in churches through the years have come out of a time volunteering together. One friendship began over fifteen years ago through a Vacation Bible School skit, and another almost twenty years ago when leading a team of teens on a mission's trip. However the Lord leads, when you are new to a church, do not hesitate to love others in your midst, and you will, in turn, find lasting friendship and connection.

23

Loving Those Who Are Difficult to Love

When I was a sophomore in high school, I ran for our school's Student Council. I think my dad was a bit worried about my over-the-top optimism that all things would going swimmingly because one morning on the way to school, he asked me if I was ready for the challenges that come with leading people. I don't remember how I responded. However, I do remember asking him if there was anything I could do to avoid the so-called challenges I might face if I land the position. *"Yes,"* he said with a sly smile. *"Avoid people."*

People can be difficult, yes. My father knew it, you know it, and there is not a soul on earth who has not encountered a difficult person. I'm not necessarily talking about the person who has regularly and deliberately hurt you, or even the ones who have caused deep fractions in relationships. Those relationships carry with them weightier issues that may need a different layer of help and assistance. But more so, I'm referring to the people we come across in our churches that we just don't like. Sometimes the reasons are because of personal attacks, but more often than not, they are for minute reasons. Maybe we don't like the way they speak out about their political views, or we don't like that they don't stop talking when you run into them, or perhaps it's a person who is especially clingy. Clearly, we're not going to have perfect chemistry with everyone in a church body, but Christ exhorts us to be unified in Him, so we can't simply ignore these people, nor we can resort to treating them unlovingly. That is one of the hardest concepts to live out as a human, but remember, difficult people are not something new to our current culture. Since the beginning of time, people have been figuring out what it means to love and interact with one another despite differences and personality conflicts.

In the book of Numbers, Moses, one of the great leaders in the Bible, laments how difficult it is to lead and love a group of very challenging people. The Israelites had complained...and complained...and complained. Though God had provided for them in miraculous ways, though He had given them manna to nourish their families, they were not satisfied. And so, they approach Moses with their wailings and share their desire for meat and other luxuries. They literally mourn over the days in Egypt (somehow forgetting the whole slavery bit) and reflect on the long-lost days when they had cucumbers, melons, leeks, onions, and garlic...and meat (Num. 11:4-6) In Egypt, they were beaten and forced into gruesome labor, but somehow that slipped their mind. Somehow their miraculous deliverance from this awful place was moved to the backburner, and they just plain wanted meat. Where was their *stinking meat?* Moses can't handle these people anymore, so in utter raw honesty and frustration he says to God:

> "Why have you dealt ill with your servant? And why have I not found favor in your sight, that you lay the burden of all this people on me? Did I conceive all this people? Did I give them birth, that you should say to me, 'Carry them in your bosom, as a nurse carries a nursing child,' to the land that you swore to give their fathers? Where am I to get meat to give to all this people? For they weep before me and say, 'Give us meat, that we may eat.' I am not able to carry all this people alone; the burden is too heavy for me. If you will treat me like this, kill me at once, if I find favor in your sight, that I may not see my wretchedness" (Num. 11:11-15)

Woah. That's the kind of real irritation that emerges when dealing with difficult people. In the last verse, Moses essentially says to God, *I can't do this. It's too much, and I've had enough.* But notice who Moses is turning to with his honest annoyances. Rather than merely lashing out at the people, Moses goes to God with his frustrations. He knows it's the only way to persevere with difficult people. No human can love someone well whom they deem frustrating, annoying, or difficult by their own strength. You can't do it!

We Love in Christ

There are three essential truths when it comes to loving difficult people, and this is the first. We must recognize that we cannot do this without Jesus. It is only *in Christ* that we're able to love someone who is not easy to love. It is only in looking to Jesus and abiding in Him that we find the ability to be gracious rather than bitter or unloving.

Paul says in Romans 13:8: "Owe no one anything, except to love each other, for the one who loves another has fulfilled the law." We can do all the religious "rituals" in the world, but if we neglect love for one another, then we are not ultimately living in obedience to God. The way we love others is a measure of our own understanding of the profundity of God's love for us. We can't claim to love God but choose to only love certain brothers or sisters in Christ. Though it's counter-intuitive, we also can't indefinitely ignore difficult people, nor should we ever talk poorly of anyone whom God has placed in our midst. We aren't expected to be close friends with everyone in our church family, but we are called to love beyond our close buddies. Listen to what Jesus says in Matthew 5:46-47: "For if you love those who love you, what reward do you have...and if you greet only your brothers, what more are you doing than others?" The idea here is not that every person we encounter in our church needs to become a close confidant, but that every person we encounter we should engage with love, and you can't love selectively or by ignoring.

In some ways, loving others in Christ takes practice. It's a sort of discipline that may be uncomfortable at times, and it might stretch us to spend an hour with someone we don't particularly get along with, but when we are pursuing someone out of obedience to Christ and love for Him, it gives us a whole new perspective. And we can trust that God will give us exactly what we need to show others the love and grace He has called us to show. The next time you see someone walking down the hallway and you want to make a beeline in the opposite direction, say a quick prayer. Ask the Lord to soften you and put a sincere sense of love for that person in your heart and watch and see what God does in you and for you.

You Are Not Immune to Being a Difficult Person!

Second, it's helpful to remember that at some point or another, you too are difficult to love. You might be the person someone else struggles to show grace to, and the likelihood is that you are, for at least one person. We can't be so oblivious to our own shortcomings that we assume we are always easy to get along with. Realizing this is one of the best remedies to loving difficult people in the church. The old adage still has merit: *put yourself in someone else's shoes.* We too quickly write someone off because of an off-handed comment or a silly response. But have you ever done or said something and later thought, "Why did I say that?" You need daily grace more than you know, so be readily willing to show it to others.

Pressing Into Difficult Relationships Causes Spiritual Growth

Third, showing mercy and kindness to others, knowing that people show it to you even when you don't realize it, causes personal and spiritual growth. We are all being sanctified, and often in ways we can't even see. The friendships in which you must fight to show love may end up being some of the richest that you have. How kind of God to help us mature spiritually when we press into the hard things He has asked us to trust Him in doing, including loving people who may be difficult. Remember that the people you have committed to in your church are not random brothers and sisters, but they are a people whom God has deliberately and purposefully put into your life.

When We Fan the Flame

Though most of our struggle with certain people in our churches is over menial things, there are times when the issues become more and more significant because the annoyances build and build. Years ago, we had a group in our church who got together weekly for community service. The interpersonal relationships had some friction, but over time the sparks started a fire. What began as differing opinions over who and how to serve turned into a name-calling, salvation-questioning disagreement that lasted for months. Unfortunately, these kinds of escalations are not uncommon when we try to ignore frustrations, when we triangulate and bring in third parties, and when we lose the focus on what we are ultimately doing and whom we are ultimately serving.

If you have someone in the church with whom a deep rift is forming, know that God is able to fill the crack. No relationship is beyond healing because of God's grace and mercy. *Not one relationship.* When tensions rise, it's crucial that we remember our shared purpose and the call to unity that Christ emphasized. Rather than allowing conflicts to fester, we should prayerfully seek reconciliation through honest conversation and with a spirit of humility. It might be that after an honest talk it makes sense to move groups or switch Sunday school classes for the sake of unity in the church, but create the space only after a conversation that attempts to bring healing and show grace. When we do this, the disagreeing can turn into times of growth and understanding. Pray urgently and boldly over these difficult relationships, connect over the common mission, and interact with humble and face-to-face dialogue.

Someone once told me that when you see a person in the church that you struggle with, remember that Christ shed His blood for them. Jesus loves them so much that He gave His life for that person. Who are we to treat them less than lovingly by thinking they are a waste of our time or energy. The world will know our love for Jesus by our love for others (John 13:35). In the grace and strength of Christ, love the difficult people in your church well.

24

Loving God's People Despite Our Insecurities

Early on in our ministry life, I tried to circulate on Sunday mornings and say "Hi" to various people sitting in the sanctuary. One Sunday, I shook hands with a woman who had had surgery the week before. "I'm sure you heard about the surgery," she said quietly. "I told your husband it was OK to let you know."

I did know she had surgery, but I didn't inquire about the details, though I acted like I was up to date on everything. Not bothering to investigate about the particulars, I looked at this woman and said, "How are you feeling?"

She responded with a hushed tone that she was doing fine but unfortunately had an "accident" the day before. I assumed she meant a car accident. What other kind of accident is there?

"Oh, I'm so sorry to hear that, but listen," I said, awkwardly trying on the part of the empathetic counselor, "I've had several accidents. I know how embarrassing it can be."

"You have?" She looked very confused, so I continued.

"I have. In fact, I had a small one not long ago. It was pretty upsetting even though it was small. I know you'll be OK but let me know if there is anything I can do to help." Then I hugged her, whisked on to the next congregant, and made a mental note that I needed to let my husband know about this poor woman's accident. When I did inform him, he in turn informed me, with simultaneous panic and laughter, that this dear congregant had *bladder surgery.* Her accidents did not involve cars. For the next several weeks, I wondered what this congregant thought of me each time I hastily slipped out of the sanctuary.

Every time we say something silly, misunderstand a conversation, or just have a very awkward chat with someone, a coin gets dropped into our bucket of insecurities. And each time, the weight becomes heavier. With the burden comes the temptation to step back just a little further from relationships in the church. I have felt this weight, shaming myself for saying dumb things like I did with the woman and her surgery. As a result, I give into Satan's lies that it just might be better to avoid getting to know people than it is to make a fool of myself. Other insecurities cause us to believe that people don't really want to get to know us anyway, so what's the point of making the effort?

What are Insecurities?

At their essence, insecurities are forms of fear. Some of these insecurities are not wrong. For example, we're naturally going to feel insecure if we're living with someone who is harming us. And we should feel a sense of insecurity when in a situation or circumstance that might be unsafe because these kinds of insecurities innately warn us that danger is near. But that's not usually the kind of insecurity that keeps us from building relationships in our churches. This kind of insecurity comes from self-doubt or a feeling of inferiority, and at the heart of this self-doubt we usually discover who or what is ultimately forming our identity.

One of my ministry colleagues recently told me a story about a Scripture reader who signed up to read one Sunday, but the reader forgot and did not show up for her slotted time in the service. She was profusely apologetic, but the ministry leader assured her it was not a big deal as someone is always readily available to fill in if needed. A few months later, the ministry leader asked her to participate in a special reading for a worship service, but she refused stating she would never again participate in any kind of reading because she could not get over the embarrassment of her forgetfulness.

Friends, this kind of insecure reaction is exactly what Satan delights in. For you to think so lowly of yourself that you believe you cannot be used by God in spite of your mistakes, is not believing that your ultimate identity is in Christ. Before you can effectively love the people of God, and in turn experience the generous love of others, you must ask yourself what determines your self-worth. It may be that the answer to that reveals hidden idols in your heart, and these idols will get in the way of building deep relationships time and time again. If approval determines your worth, then when someone does not respond to your well-thought-out message in a timely matter, you may begin to spiral with anxiety. If looking like you have it together determines your self-worth, you will never experience the freedom of vulnerability with brothers and sisters in Christ.

How Insecurities Can Become a Hindrance

Being overly uncertain about ourselves can hurt our personal relationships within a church, but it can also affect the church body at large because we will often avoid personal conversations or step back from serving. These become roadblocks in our ability to love others, and the church cannot function in loving God and loving each other if we are all primarily consumed with ourselves. I remember one Sunday, my teen daughter said to me as I was heading out the door, "Mom, you're wearing *that* to church?" I spent the entire morning thinking almost exclusively about my outfit and how it may or may not appear to others. How many people did I avoid meaningful conversations with that Sunday because I thought my dress looked weird? And how much of the sermon did I miss because I kept thinking of the ways I should have changed the outfit? It's comical, really, but this is what happens when we hand over the reins to our insecurities. The ride is wild and selfish. There is not a person who does not struggle with insecurity in some form or another, but if we don't confess it, and ask the Lord to help us with it, the church can be affected.

The Antidote to Our Insecurities

The more we begin to grasp what it means that our identity is in Christ, the more willingly and eagerly we will love on God's people in our midst. Jesus Himself is not ashamed to have you in His family. Hebrews 2:11 says, "For he who sanctifies and those who are sanctified all have one source. That is why he is not ashamed to call them brothers." Jesus delights in you. He gave His life for you, and is never ashamed of you, no matter how insecure you may feel. It is not that we are worthy in and of ourselves. The antidote to loving despite our insecurities is not to repeat over and over "I am exceptional." That just leads to pride and confidence in the flesh, and ultimately, it will not help because we are not always exceptional. Our worth comes from nothing and no one else except for Christ and His work on our behalf. As much as we long for affirmation in this life, imagine your heavenly Father who is singing loud praises over you (Zeph. 3:17) because He loves you. No earthly accolade can compare! Praise God that Jesus loves you so much that you have been made righteous in Christ. Now, go forth, in that joy and confidence, and extend His love to others in your church community.

25

Cultivating a Love for God's People in Young Children

A friend in our church recently handed me a letter that she found written by my mother to her mother. By the time we found the letter, both of these dear saints had passed away, but it was inspiring to read the penned words of a beautiful, intergenerational friendship that remained for many years. Mom wrote these words to Barbara, a woman nearly twenty-five years her senior:

> *"It is a unique opportunity I have had to sing and serve the Lord with you as a silly 5th grader, a giggling 8th grader, a "know it all" high schooler, "cool" college student, a Seminary student's wife, and then to come back…as the Pastor's wife at the church where you attend.…Through all the stages of life, I have watched you and noted above all your faithfulness in serving the God that you love. There are very few examples of people who do not grow weary and give up, but you have continued year after year serving joyfully. Your living testimony has been there for me when I feel like giving up…"*

As I read these words, that last line especially struck me: "*Your living testimony has been there for me when I feel like giving up.*" Mom learned from Barbara as a child simply by watching her through the years, and God used that example to cultivate in her an understanding of what it means to love and serve God's church. This is exactly how we instill love for others in our children. Kids learn what it is to love God and love others by our example. Parent, like everything we've touched on when it comes to loving and embracing God's church, you cannot cultivate in your child a willingness to love others if you are not putting in the effort yourself. And if you feel it, that sentence is not intended to produce guilt. Like one of my friends used to say, "Blessed is the man who never stops starting over." Jesus knows the desires of your heart, and if part of that desire is to earnestly love God's people in the way God has commanded us to love, then He will help you do it. He will also give you the strength to start again in the times you fail. Your kids will observe that pattern, and they will learn from it.

Teaching Love by Exemplifying Love

Because they learn by example, don't hesitate to involve your children when you are loving God's people by getting to know others in the church. For example, if you're learning names, have your child with you when you introduce yourself, and later, quiz each other on the names, and ask them what they remember about your new acquaintance. Your child will learn from you that remembering personal details is a way of showing love when you're new to a congregation. When you have people into your home, have your kids eat with you so they also can get to know the other adults in the church. This is one of the greatest ways to make the church body feel more like an extended family. And simultaneously, they will learn from you that sometimes loving others involves giving of your time and resources. And you never know what adults in the church might end up being your child's mentor. You never know whose example God is using even now to teach your child in the way that Barbara taught my mom through her "living testimony." Give them opportunities to observe and learn from other people in the church whether that's during corporate worship or a meal around your table.

Unfortunately, our kids also learn from our sinful example. Thank God for His never-ending grace and His powerful work in our children even when we are weak. But we must "never stop starting over" by repenting of the times we are two-faced in our love for others. We can't cultivate a love for others in our children if we're not teaching them what it is to love each other in our own home. If we regularly talk badly about our spouse in front of our kids, but then try to teach them the importance of loving other Christians, they will quickly see the discrepancy and learn from our hypocrisy. The same is true for people in the church we have a hard time with. It's one thing to honestly empathize with our kids when they are annoyed by someone, but it's quite another to let them hear you talk trash about someone. When we do this, our children learn that if we don't like someone, talking badly about them is OK. Telling your child that you understand what it is to be frustrated with people can certainly be helpful. But don't leave it at that. Talk them through what it looks like to love someone because they are made in the image of God. Help them to see the ways that God has loved them and ask your child what they can learn about loving others from God's great love.

Teaching Love Through Natural Connectedness

Not only do kids learn what it is to love others in the church by example, but they develop friendships simply by being with other kids in the church. This happens through children's church, Sunday Schools, Vacation Bible Schools, and anywhere that the kids of the church are together on a regular basis. And here's what's beautiful. In the church, they are cultivating friendships and learning what it looks like to befriend others who may be different from them in a setting that is centered around biblical teaching, and from believers who are wanting your child to better understand Jesus. What better environment is there to learn what it looks like to love one another?

Our kids naturally grow in their love for each other by having fun together, by learning about God together, and, hopefully, by serving together. Many relationships in the church form at young ages and remain strong even into adulthood, and sometimes these relationships are what keeps a teen coming back later. When my daughter was in elementary school, the church we attended was small, and there was only one other child in her grade. However, there was a girl just below her in age, so she and my daughter spent all sorts of time together, and we fostered that relationship by involving her in various children's ministries with this friend. When my daughter entered high school, she did not love attending youth group, but she had grown to love this friend through the years, so going to youth group was not a huge battle because her buddy also attended. This friend has remained steadfast in my daughter's life through the years, even standing as a bridesmaid at her wedding. The time with other children in the church is not insignificant in their cultivation of love for others. They come together with a diverse group from differing schools and backgrounds and cultures and learn about God together while simultaneously understanding what is to love together. It's truly beautiful.

It's amazing to me that this woman, Barbara, who taught my mom by example when she was a child, ended up serving alongside mom and dad when my father became the pastor at Barbara's church. My mom ended her letter to Barbara with these words: *"Your constant faithfulness, I know, will continue to minister to me and to encourage my own faithfulness as we together serve in Christ's church which he loves so deeply and for which he gave his life."* Barbara became a rock for my mom, even serving mom in her last days on earth. May we be this same kind of faithful example and show the love of God to others so that one day our children might grow to understand, through His church, how wide and how long and how high and how deep is the love of Christ (Eph. 3:18).

26

Cultivating a Love for God's People in Teens

"*Mom, I was kinda freaking out. She just kept talking to me, and I didn't know what to do!*" I laughed inwardly as my young teen described an encounter with an adult congregant after worship one Sunday. The woman in our church was merely asking my daughter about a recent trip she took, but you would have thought my teen had been cornered by a banshee. I've been around teens enough to know that many are like my daughter and would happily avoid interaction with anyone outside of their peers on a Sunday morning. This is normal, and you probably felt similarly at this age even if you don't entirely remember it. Even so, these are teachable moments with our teens in which we can explain the beauty of the church being their extended family. I remind my teen often that the same men and women who inquire about her trips or extra-curricular activities are the same men and women who were there for her when her parents were both sick with COVID, when she lost her grandma, and they are the same people who stepped in with practical needs when mom and dad traveled overseas for a mission's trip. Our church is an extended family, so we must teach this to cultivate in our teens a love for God's people. But for our teens to learn to *express love*, they need to *feel loved* by others in the church.

This is one of the main reasons that teens should be involved in corporate worship and not have a separate youth service during the church's time of worship. Many churches have separated teens to make their services more youth friendly, and

I certainly understand the sentiment, but how do we teach our teens that worship is not about them if we're creating a worship service that is exclusively for them? And how do we teach our teens what it looks like to love and be loved intergenerationally if they don't regularly interact with others during worship who are younger and older? I still remember those in my church who showed an interest in me as a teenager. I will never forget one couple in particular who came to one of my high school basketball games. To this day, I can recall feeling so loved by these people who cared enough about me to come and cheer me on. And then when I saw them at Sunday morning worship, I was eager to say hi and tell them how the basketball season was going. *Experiencing* that love as a teen was integral in helping me better understand what it means to *show* love to God's people.

Equally important for our teens is that we, as parents, view our local church as an extended family. It's going to be more difficult to teach your teen what it looks like to love God's people if you don't see them as a group worth loving in tangible, family-like ways. If your family arrives late and slips out immediately after the sermon, you're not treating the body like you would your family, eager to see them and hear how they're doing. If your church is so large that no one knows you and your family, then your attendance can too easily become an item to check off the "to-do" list, rather than a commitment to serve and love a body of believers under the Lordship of Christ.

Ephesians 2:19 says that "you are no longer strangers and aliens, but you are fellow citizens with the saints and **members of the household of God.**" The church in this verse is not described as a thing to go and do, but it is described as who you *are*. You are part of God's family. The church was started with the apostles, and by the Spirit it spread throughout Jerusalem, Judea, Samaria, and to the ends of the earth. And that building continues with you and your family, brick by brick, with Christ as the one who holds it all together. Your teens need to understand that they are a part of this ongoing work as a member of God's household. When your family experiences church as a group of people who become your mothers and fathers and brothers and sisters, it becomes easier to teach our teens why and how we show genuine love and care for people in our churches.

Since this is not always something that comes naturally for teens, having conversations about what the Bible means by "loving one another" is important. Maybe make this the focus of a few of your family devotions together. Choose a verse where the Bible commands us to love, and then ask your teen questions about what that looks like in a very practical, concrete situation.

John 13:35 says that we will be known as Christ followers by our love for one another. That can be intimidating to read because sincere love can be hard for many – including our teens. But it's how the world will know that we are Christians. In the same way that a house has distinguished markers as a "house," love is the characteristic that distinguishes you as a Christians – it marks you as a Christ Follower. And in the same way that it's often difficult to love our siblings, it can also be difficult to love some in the house of God. Talk to your teens about ways that God has helped you when it comes to loving people you are easily frustrated with. What has the Lord taught you that you can pass on to your teens regarding kids in the youth group who might annoy them or who ignore them? These are real situations in the church. We, as adults, know we can't quit a congregation every time someone in our church dismisses us or acts meanly to us, so how do you encourage your teen in the same way? Quitting youth group is not always the answer because they will inevitably encounter another believer in their life who they will again struggle with. Talk with your teens, and ask them questions such as: What does it look like to show love to a Sunday School teacher they don't connect with? What does it look like to love the lady in the congregation who is long-winded? We all struggle with these kinds of scenarios, so talk, empathize, and together pray, asking the Spirit to help you and your teen to better understand what it looks like to love one another in the body of Christ.

I remember receiving a letter from a teen several years back. This three-page letter included some of the most meaningful words I've ever read. The teenager explained how my willingness to show interest in her giftedness was life-changing, and my encouraging words throughout her teen years were both an example and just what she needed to continue to pursue her area of interest. Friends, I had no idea the kind of impact I was having on this teen until I read her letter. I was taken aback by how significant my words of encouragement were to her, and I was moved by God's faithfulness through her to me. While God was working in me during a few very trying years, He was also using me, even when I didn't see it, and I learned that through this young woman's encouraging words.

I've told my kids about this letter, only to explain that these kinds of words from them as teenagers can mean the world to an adult. They can have as great of an impact in the body of Christ as any single adult can. If your teen appreciates someone in the church, encourage them to find that person on a Sunday, and *tell them*. If your teen thinks another adult is "just really cool to talk to," as one of my teens once said, encourage them to thank that congregant for the way they listen so well. When we're doing this, we're sharpening one another – across generations, and ages, and stages of life - and this kind of love is profound and can have a deep impact on the church at large. Adults, love. Children, love. Teens, love. We must, by His grace and with His strength extend the love to the body of believers that Christ has so readily shown to us.

PART FIVE:
Serving God's People:
The Importance of Helping Our Church Family

But whoever would be great among you must be your servant, and whoever would be first among you must be your slave, even as the Son of Man came not to be served but to serve, and to give his life as a ransom for many.

Matthew 20:26b-28

27

What Keeps Us from Serving?

What compels a church attender to give up time in their already busy schedule to serve in the church? I asked myself this question while ambling around our empty sanctuary one afternoon. I'd been working on a written announcement regarding an event at the church, one that required many hands to be successful. As I formed the words, there was a tone of plea in them, and I wondered why I felt the need to compel people to *please help.* Does the church ask too much of people who are already so busy?

Research shows that approximately 42 per cent of churchgoers volunteer in their churches, and about 27 per cent in their communities.[1] There are many reasons for the low numbers of willing people to serve in their churches and communities, but perhaps the most significant reason is that we've lost sight of why it is that we serve as Christians.

If you ask a believer in Christ why they *should* serve, you'd probably get a variety of answers. Some might say they serve because it's rewarding and fulfilling, and others might say that they serve simply because they feel compelled (from, say, an announcement that became an over-the-top plea). Some might admit that they feel good when they serve because they are doing something morally helpful, checking off the "good deed" box. Though these are fine responses, not any of these are the

1.   https://research.lifeway.com/2023/05/12/bridging-the-gap-between-church-service-and-community-service/#:~:text=A%20recent%20Lifeway%20Research%20study,27%25%20volunteer%20in%20their%20communities.

reasons that Jesus calls us to serve. The reality is, service is not always rewarding, and we only become disgruntled if we do it simply because we feel guilty from a plea.

The primary reason that we give of our talents, our time, and our energy is *because of Jesus.* Your love for your Savior is manifested in your selfless deeds toward others. In 1 John 3:18, we are reminded that we should "not love in word or talk but in deed and in truth." So, don't just talk about love, practice it because in doing so, you are expressing love for your heavenly Father. Ultimately, serving is not about the outward act but our inward heart being inclined toward God. When you lend a hand to someone in your neighborhood who needs help, you are serving Jesus. When you bring a meal to someone in need, you are serving Jesus. When you teach a children's Sunday school class, you are serving Jesus. Do you see the profundity of this?

And Jesus set the example for us when it comes to service. His life on earth consistently prioritized the needs of others over His own needs, regularly demonstrating humility and compassion. The ultimate act of service is seen in His sacrifice on the cross when He paid – in full – for our sins. What other response is there but to serve and love others as an extension of the underserving love that is shown to us.

In a sermon back in 1906, author and pastor J.R. Miller said these powerful words about serving: "If we would learn to serve as Christ did – it would make us think of others around us, not as those from whom we may get some gain, exact some attention or promotion – but as those to whom we may impart some good, render some service."[2] When we lose sight of what serving is ultimately about, we back away from it because we don't think it will satisfy us, or we lose our motivation because we're merely answering a plea or looking for accolades. Service

---

2.   https://www.sermonindex.net/modules/articles/index.
php?view=article&aid=32519

is not about filling a time slot, but it embodies what it means to love Jesus.

Excuses for Not Serving

Even so, many Christians excuse themselves from serving for a variety of reasons. One of the most common I've heard is that they "don't feel called." While it's certainly true that the Holy Spirit prompts us as a means to guide and direct, it's too easy to use a lack of "calling" as an excuse to not serve. It's a curious excuse because our calling, according to Scripture, is to love God with all our heart and to love our neighbor as ourselves (Matt. 22:37-39). What we really mean when we say that we don't feel called to serve in a particular area is that the kind of service being asked of us makes us feel uncomfortable; we don't feel a natural leaning toward it. We'll delve more into serving outside our comfort zones, but think for a moment with me about the number of people in Scripture God called to serve in a very uncomfortable way. I think immediately of Mary. God called her to carry the Son of God, and to tell Joseph that she was pregnant though she was a virgin. Who would readily volunteer for that job? Not many...because it's uncomfortable. And yet, God called her to it.

Another common excuse to not serve, especially in the behind-the-scenes areas of church life, is that serving can be thankless. I remember years ago arriving early to church on a Sunday morning to find that chairs were not put away from an event the night before. I began folding and stacking the chairs, and with each one my grumbling became more pronounced, and the folding of the chair clanged louder until I called out to no one, "this isn't my job!" Had someone been standing there, applauding my efforts, I probably would have done it gladly. My heart was filled with such pride, that I had the idea that putting chairs away was somehow beneath me. It was a thankless job that no one would see, and I was mad because of it.

Colossians 3:22-24 says, "Bondservants, obey in everything those who are your earthly masters, not by way of eye-service, as people-pleasers, but with sincerity of heart, fearing the Lord. Whatever you do, work heartily, as for the Lord and not for men, knowing that from the Lord you will receive the inheritance as your reward. You are serving the Lord Christ." Believers in Jesus, we serve not for the purpose of an earthly reward. It's pride that has seeped into our service when we become tired of giving of our time because of lack of praise. I know one pastor's wife who combats this by going up to church when no one is there and cleaning the bathrooms. She does this as a reminder that *all service* is done unto the Lord, and *all service* is worthy of our time and energy because *all service* brings glory to God when it is done for Jesus.

Of course, desiring approval is natural. It's the way God made us. But this is exactly what Paul addresses when he speaks to the New Testament servants in Colossae. If they are not appreciated by their masters, they can either start doing the minimum out of frustration, or they can keep in mind that their ultimate master is Christ, and He will one day reward their faithfulness. That is sure and certain. Jesus sees you when you're washing the coffee pots after a Sunday service. He sees you when you're putting away the chairs before and after worship. He sees you when you wash the sheets in the nursery's cribs. He sees you when you take an hour to help fold bulletins. Our heavenly Father sees our service and delights in it when we serve to bring Him glory.

The last, but most common excuse to not serve is overcommitment. One mother said to me that they were taking a break from doing anything in their church because they were so busy with their kid's activities and other work obligations. They would go when they could on Sundays, but they just needed to step back from the church "or else we might drown." As I've referenced earlier, I do empathize with the mother's dire comment, and overcommitment can become an issue that negatively affects you and your family. But the problem is that we cannot remove ourselves from responsibilities in the church because serving one another is an expected part of the Christian life. If you're overcommitted, something may need to go, but the answer is not to dismiss the needs around you because "you're too busy." That is not to say that we can't overcommit in areas of service, and we need to be careful with that. Sometimes we volunteer in *too* many areas, taking spots that could (and maybe should) be filled with others in the church. But not serving at all because of busyness is just not an option for a Christian because it's through willing hands and feet that God's church functions.

Friends, the reality is, the church cannot do what it is meant to do without volunteers willing to serve the body, and it cannot be an effective witness to His gospel when the reason for serving is misunderstood. As we explore the various elements to service, may the Lord give us open hearts and hands, willing to serve Him by serving His church.

28

Serving Outside of Your Comfort Zone

A local church is not fulfilling its part of the mission to display the gospel of Jesus if it does not have an outward focus. We can become too comfortable becoming consumeristic within the walls of the church, and we can also become too comfortable with the ease of our Christian circles and so neglect relationships outside the walls of the church. You are a light in this dark world, believer (Matt. 5:14). In the same way that our eyes are drawn to light when a room is dark, unbelievers will be drawn to the work of Jesus in you, but we need to be deliberate about putting ourselves in places where this light can shine.

A few years back, a woman in our church asked to get together for coffee, and during our time together, she expressed feeling very apathetic in her faith. My heart was heavy for this young woman as I could see the visible marks of a woman worn physically and emotionally. Thinking back on times in my life when I felt dry spiritually, I asked this young woman when the last time was that she did something that stretched her faith. She admitted that it had been a long time since doing something that required great faith and trust in God. I asked her this question because of an experience I had in my thirties when I went through a season of feeling distant from God and His people. In God's providence, I was approached about leading a mission's trip to New York City. I felt ill-equipped, it was not an easy time to leave, and I knew it would be exhausting. I said yes, but only with certain stipulations. A few things had to fall right into place, things that I was sure would not, and if they didn't, I would not go. But God removed every obstacle, and as I experienced that happening, my faith was revigorated. And the trip itself, though I was stretched in every way, renewed my relationship with Jesus in unexpected and necessary ways.

Serving Inside the Church in a Way that Stretches You

Sometimes, the best remedy for our sense of disconnectedness spiritually is doing something that requires a great amount of faith in God. 1 Peter 4:10-11 says, "As each has received a gift, use it to serve one another...whoever serves, as one who serves by the strength that God supplies..." Peter reminds God's people here that when we serve, we do so *by God's strength*. We can't understand what that truly means until we serve beyond our comforts and experience the Lord's provisions in doing so. Serving outside our comfort zone forces us to shed the pride that "we've got this," and causes us to do what we should do every time we serve – rely on Jesus to do what He's called us to do.

Serving strengthens the body of Christ, and this can (and should) happen both inside and outside the church. Internally, it's so easy to limit our service to what is "easy," but we're not stretching our faith enough to see God work when we lean back and do something that requires very little of us. Many are willing to serve by writing a check; fewer will come out on a Saturday and volunteer at a children's event. Many are willing to bring a snack with them on a Sunday morning; fewer are willing to give up a few hours to help clean after the service. Where is there a need in your church that will stretch you because it will cause you to very deliberately trust the Lord to provide creativity, time, or resources that you feel you don't have? When the Holy Spirit moves you to say yes to a need, ask the Lord to provide exactly what you need to do the job, and watch and see how He works. God may provide in unexpected ways, but He makes us capable to do what He's called us to do.

I remember one year being asked to participate in a drama for Vacation Bible School. I was newly married and ready to serve in my church, but not it this way. There was a need, though, as the person committed dropped out at the last minute, and I really had no reason to say "no" other than, if I was being honest, I really didn't want to spend my whole morning at church Bible camp. I knew that wasn't the best reason to decline, so I nervously agreed, and I recall asking the Lord to help me with two specific things: 1) I was afraid of being self-conscious with the goofy part I was playing in front of the other adults, so I asked Jesus to help me not concern myself with what others thought; 2) I was afraid of not remembering the lines, so I asked Jesus to help me remember the parts where I was sharing gospel truth. Not only did the Lord reveal Himself by helping me in these two specific ways, but *I had so much fun.* In fact, to this day I write VBS dramas, and I never would have dipped my toes into this kind of writing had I not said yes to this small area of service.

Serving Outside the Church in a Way that Stretches You

The internal ministries grow and become vibrant when many hands are doing the work, and simultaneously the Lord gives us renewed zeal for Him as we experience the unique ways the Lord provides when serving in areas where we're not necessarily comfortable. And the same is true when it comes to serving outside of the church. Mission's trips are common ways that churches answer the necessary call to service, and they are a great way of strengthening connectedness with other believers while serving outside our comfort zone. Every Christian should go on one mission's trip at some point in their life to see and experience what Jesus is doing around the globe and to stretch our sometimes-narrow view of the world. *However,* sometimes it can be easier to say yes to a week or month out of the country than it can be to give regularly of our time and energy as a light in our own communities. Start here, believers. Every church should offer ways for its body to go out and serve, and their offerings are a great way to get plugged in to local missions. Utilize that connection and go. Serve. Whether it's a food pantry, a homeless shelter, or a monthly hands-on project that helps neighbors in need; these may be some of the most uncomfortable ways of serving, but they can also be some of the most formative and profound.

Spiritual growth happens when we stretch ourselves and do what we would not "typically" do, and this includes sharing the gospel with those whom we serve. It's too easy to minimize service to simply our presence among the needy, but presence alone does not fulfill the great commission to "go make disciples of all nations..." (Matt. 28:19). This is the evangelism aspect of service which is a necessary for all followers of Christ. Is it uncomfortable? It certainly can be, but we can't excuse evangelism away because we're not good at it, because it makes us nervous, or because we don't think it's our "giftedness."

Are some uniquely gifted for evangelism? Yes. But all Christians are called to be disciple makers. You know what motivates you to share the good news of Jesus? Being around other believers who love to share the gospel. We just spent an evening with one of those people, and his zeal for Jesus and desire to share what God has done is contagious, and I felt compelled by the Spirit's work in him. Find people like this in your church and ask them to get together to pray or to hold you accountable in a relationship where you have felt reluctant or embarrassed to share your belief in Jesus.

Serving inside and outside the walls of the church in ways that may make us uncomfortable pushes us to grow stronger in our faith. That spiritual maturing not only connects us more intimately to our Savior, but it also strengthens our connectedness to each other as we serve alongside our brothers and sisters. The church, as a whole, is strengthened by your willingness to serve in ways that stretch your faith. And when you experience the power of God firsthand as he provides what is necessary for your service, bear testimony to what He has done. The Holy Spirit can use what you learn as you serve others as a way to prompt another brother or sister toward doing the same. Our relationship with Jesus is deepened when we're willing to be uncomfortable and serve. Those whom we serve are strengthened by your love and your witness. And other believers may grow by your testimony of God's great work in your own life when you answered the call to serve. It's a beautifully profound cycle. Jesus set the example, friends, when He came not to be served by to serve (Matt. 20:28). May we continue to be a people who follow that example and find delight in taking risks for the sake of the gospel and for the sake of His church.

29

Serving by Utilizing Your Gifts

After the Warner Brothers movie, *Barbie,* came out in 2023, Billie Eilish's song, *What Was I Made For?* became an instant hit. The lyrics to the first verse go like this:

I used to float, now I just fall down
I used to know but I'm not sure now
What I was made for
What was I made for?

The song is a reflection on belonging and identity, and the melancholy tune begs for an answer to the question we all ask at one point or another: *What is my purpose?* One sixty-eight-year-old woman wrote this in response to Eilish's lyrics: "This song asks the question that I have (struggled) with for all of my 68 years...I thought I had the answer several times, only to realize that it slipped through my fingers yet again."[1] Apart from Jesus, believer, we will keep searching for the answer to this question our entire life, and every time we think we've found the purpose, it will inevitably slip through our fingers. But when Jesus opens our eyes to Him, our purpose could not be clearer. Listen to these rich words from Ephesians 2:10: "For we are his workmanship, created in Christ Jesus for good works, which God prepared beforehand, that we should walk in them." God saves us not just *from* something, but He saves us *for* something. We are the workmanship of God, and that

---

1. https://www.today.com/popculture/music/billie-eilish-what-was-i-made-for-song-meaning-lyrics-rcna136724

word in the original language is *poiema* which literally means "that which is made."[2] We are God's amazing and breathtaking work of art, and He created us "for good works." You want to understand what you were made for, believer? Here it is in Ephesians. You have been raised to new life, as a masterpiece created by God, to do good work for His glory, work that God prepared for us to do before we were even born. In sum, *the service we do for others, carried out in Christ's strength and for His glory, is what we were made for.*

It's interesting to me that we're surprised by the joy and satisfaction that often come when we volunteer our time and talent. When you read this verse in Ephesians, that result makes sense. Each one of us is gifted by God uniquely. *Each one.* Understand that when God created you, the masterpiece that He put together included very specific giftedness. He did not forget a single gift or talent when He created each masterpiece. You may feel that God looked over you when you compare yourself with others but doing that is futile. We weren't made to live life glancing sideways, but to look up asking our heavenly father to reveal our unique giftedness and to use it to advance His kingdom.

Not only are you valuable to God, who created you, but you are valuable to your church because of the ways God has gifted you. A few chapters later in Ephesians, Paul lists some of the individual giftedness within a church body. Why does God gift people with varying talents? Chapter 4 verse 12 answers this: "To equip the saints for the work of ministry, for building up the body of Christ..." The various gifts represented help the church; they build her up. The question many want answered is, if God has uniquely gifted me, then how do I discern that spiritual giftedness?

---

2.   John R. Stott, *The Message of Ephesians: The Bible Speaks Today.* (Downers Grove, IL.:Inter-Varsity Press, 1979) p.84.

Discerning Giftedness

First, it's important to understand that the lists that Paul offers in Ephesians 4 and 1 Corinthians 12 can't be used as excuses not to serve. In other words, it's easy to take these lists and say that I'm not going to serve because ___ is not my spiritual gift. The more important perspective is: *This is an area where I can serve; now let me see how I can use my spiritual gift of ___ to help them out.* Do you see the difference? Almost every one of our gifts can and would be welcomed in an area of service to the church.

There are several ways to discern our specific giftedness, and the first, perhaps the most important, is to pray for wisdom and understanding. To be clear, this is not what to do as a "last resort" when discerning giftedness. This is the first thing we should do because it's the most important route in discovering our spiritual gifts. God promises to grant wisdom when you ask of Him (James 1:5-8), so ask expectantly and boldly! And beyond seeking understanding of your own gifts, pray for the needs in your church that require willing hands and hearts. Pray that the Lord will raise up the people needed to fulfill the jobs that need to be done and ask the Lord boldly if there is an area where you might be helpful, even when you're not totally clear if it's something you're "good" at.

To that end, another way to discern spiritual giftedness is simply by serving. 1 Peter 4:10 says, "As each has received a gift, use it to serve one another, as good stewards of God's varied grace". Sometimes, God reveals your spiritual gifts through your service, so you don't have to wait to serve until you fully understand your giftedness. Peter says in this verse, serve one another knowing that you have been given a gift.

Sometimes we volunteer in an area where we think we are gifted, and we find that we really enjoy what we're doing. This is one of the kind ways that God reveals the way He has uniquely gifted you. But be wise in asking other trusted leaders whether they sense the same giftedness. We once had a young woman who desired to serve in our children's ministry, and we were delighted! She believed she had a specific gift in teaching children, but after a few observed her, it was clear that she did not. The lessons were, quite frankly, painful, very lengthy, and not on a level that a child could understand. The pastor met with her to discuss her giftedness, and it turns out that she was so nervous in teaching the children that she had trouble focusing on anything else in preparation for the lesson. Could she have learned and improved? Absolutely. Did God use her efforts in spite of her weakness? We can know that for certain. But had she tapped into her specific giftedness? It didn't seem so. The pastor showed her the myriads of other ways to serve in children's ministry, and it turns out she was very gifted with administration. She loved organizing the children's events and ordering curriculums, and our church was blessed by her years of service in this very specific way. Serve willingly, consider how you feel about it personally, and then ask some trusted friends and leaders what they think about your perceived giftedness. This is one of the pathways the Lord uses to reveal our unique set of gifts. Serving can be the pathway to discovering what you are good at doing.

When thinking about your spiritual giftedness, reflect on this. As the Lord reveals to you the ways he has uniquely gifted you, consider that God has masterfully made you with specific talents and abilities. That masterpiece that God purposefully created is the way that He supplies for the needs of His people. The church functions and the gospel is spread *because of your gifts and your willingness to use them.* It's what you were made for, believer.

30

Serving Children in the Local Church

At my daughter's college graduation, the commencement speaker said something that has stuck with me: "Serving and teaching children is harder than you may think and way more rewarding than you might expect." During my years as a schoolteacher, I taught mostly high school students, though I occasionally dipped my toes in the very curious and strange world of Junior High. But eighth grade was as young as I would teach, and even that felt like a stretch for me, so I said no every time there was a need in children's ministry. Until, that is, I had the brilliant idea of starting a Sunday night children's program at our very young and newly-planted church. My husband matched my enthusiasm as he listened to my ideas, and then looked at me and said: "*This is great! Why don't you lead it?*" Well, shoot. But I really had no reason not to during that season of life. I will tell you that stepping out of my comfort and serving the children of our church for several years was, indeed, the hardest but most unexpectedly rewarding service I have done in the church thus far. Along with the many benefits that come from serving children, there are important reasons that every believer should consider some form of service to the kids in their church.

Jesus Set the Example

I know many willingly and quite emphatically avoid serving in the children's ministry of their churches because I've talked with church leaders who share the common struggle of obtaining volunteers in their children's ministry. Why should we care about serving these littles? *Because Jesus cares about them*. Mark 10:13-16 is the most visible place we see Jesus welcome and delight in children:

> "And they were bringing children to [Jesus] that he might touch them, and the disciples rebuked them. But when Jesus saw it, he was indignant and said to them, 'Let the children come to me; do not hinder them, for to such belongs the kingdom of God. Truly, I say to you, whoever does not receive the kingdom of God like a child shall not enter it.' And he took them in his arms and blessed them, laying his hands on them."

The disciples shooed away the moms and dads who were desperate for Jesus to simply put a hand on their child, and this makes Jesus *indignant*. The children coming to Him were essential parts of God's kingdom; in fact, He chastises the disciples because of their dismissiveness toward the little ones. Then, our Savior gathers them in His arms and blesses each one. And it's not insignificant that the children *wanted* to be with Him. Jesus set the example of tender and sincere care for kids. He doesn't do this out of duty or because it's His "job." He genuinely cares for these children and wants to bless them. It's truly beautiful. The children in our church deserve a lesson that is thought through and not just thrown together at the last minute. They deserve our sincere care for them individually and not just as a group of random kids. They deserve our love and service because Jesus Himself believes they are worthy of it. He set the example, reminding us of their significance in God's kingdom.

Many People Come to Know Jesus as a Child

Another reason we should consider serving the children in the church is because statistics show that many kids come to know Jesus at an early age. Parents have the greatest impact on a child's faith, but that does not take away from the importance of the ministries of the church that serve children. One surveyed a group of adult ministry leaders, ones faithfully serving in their church, who were asked which programs in their church they attended as a child. The results "confirmed the role of ministry programs in [a child's] faith journey: 86 per cent said Sunday School, and 59 per cent Vacation Bible School."[1] What we do in the church to serve the children matters as many come to faith through children's ministries, and, by God's grace, continue serving themselves into adulthood.

We Learn When We Teach

I didn't plan to be an English major. I had hoped to do something with music, but when that didn't pan out, I went the route of studying writing and literature simply because I felt more comfortable with those subjects than with any others. That degree led me to my first job as a high school writing teacher.

When I accepted the job, writing was not a passion. In fact, it wasn't even particularly enjoyable. But something happened when it became my responsibility to instruct students in the process of writing. When I was forced to think through how I could make a seemingly boring subject into something thrilling, my own excitement for the process was awakened. After teaching the subject for one year, I fell in love with writing.

My experience is not unusual: many teachers bear testimony to subject matters "clicking" when they teach them. When I study a passage of Scripture to teach it to our ladies' Bible study, my excitement about that section of Scripture is heightened because the learning process opens my eyes in new and fresh ways. When we teach children even the most basic truths of the Scriptures, it's so amazing how much *we* learn, both in our preparation, but also in our communication. Don't discount

---

1.   https://ministry-to-children.com/childrens-ministry-statistics/#kidmin

how much you will learn about gospel truths when you serve by teaching the children in your church.

Serving Children is Hospitable

Serving the children in the church is an act of hospitality. We don't often know these little ones well, and yet we offer our time, talent, and energy to get to know them and to make them feel welcomed in the body of believers. Hebrews 13:1-2 affirms that this "stranger" love is exactly what the Bible exhorts us to when it encourages a friendly and open welcoming of one another. When we kneel to a child's level, give them a welcoming smile, and ask them their name, we are extending the love of Christ. This kind of hospitality is so needed in the church, and when it's shown to children, it can have lasting effects.

By extension, when we show hospitality to our children, we are also showing it to their parents. When I lead our children's choir, I will often look at a child who is speaking and think of their parents. Some may be going through divorce, others trying to make it as a single parent, and a few just so tired from running the hamster wheel. Many of these burdens are represented amongst the parents of the kids you teach. Because of this, remember that when you serve the children in your church and show them genuine love, you are deeply loving their parents as well, many of whom carry large burdens.

Children Teach us So Much

In the passage from Mark 10 when Jesus welcomes the children, He says, "Truly, I say to you, whoever does not receive the kingdom of God like a child shall not enter it." Jesus points to the children as examples praising not their child*ish* faith but their child*like* faith. It's the kind of faith that a child has in a parent where there is so much trust that they run unabashedly into the arms of mom or dad when they see them. The disciples were to learn from this!

Beyond the sometimes-funny comments and silly stories that can be a joyful part of serving them, children teach us so much through their honesty, insights, and questions. Before teaching a song related to Noah's Ark a couple of years ago, I played a little three-minute cartoon video about the story. One child in the classroom looked distraught, and after the video was over, she said quietly, "You mean, all those people and all those animals drowned?" Her tenderness forced me to take a step back and reconsider the aspects of this story that are, frankly, quite dreadful. I was ready to teach a light-hearted song about animals on the ark, but we all needed some time to sit in the sadness of what happened outside the boat. It was an important lesson for me.

Serving children in the church can be hard, it can be trying, and it can often take a lot of energy. *But it is so rewarding.* This is not a call to mere babysitting, but it is an investment in the next generation of the church who needs to hear the gospel, to know the love of Jesus, and to understand that they are a significant part of the body of Christ.

31

Serving Teens in the Local Church

When my son turned eighteen, my husband invited a small group of men to join him and my son for a nice, celebratory steak dinner. The small group invited included men who had influenced my son over the course of his eighteen years and who were eager to impart wisdom and godly advice as our teen entered the new stage of adulthood. When I reflect on what my husband told me about that evening, I'm so moved by how much that time meant to my son, but what's even more touching is the various representation of men which included family, our son's former youth leader, a father-like friend from church, and a grandfatherly-like friend from church. At various stages and in differing seasons, all these men acted as extended family by reaching out and caring for my son in ways that have made a big impact on him.

Believer in Christ, the teens in your church need you. Not all teens will admit this, but I know it's true because I've observed it, and I've experienced it. To serve them is sometimes admittedly messy, but this group in our church needs our willing hands and hearts so immensely. If we truly care about raising up new leaders and servants in God's church, then we must be pouring into the teens in our midst.

Serving Teens in the Youth Ministry

Whether you are a small group leader, a praying partner, hosting a youth event, or just adding an adult presence during Sunday school, the youth ministry in your church needs volunteers ready and willing to serve the teens. Friends, this is such a critical stage of life, and if we desire to pass down our faith and cultivate in our young people a love for the church, then we must be willing to walk alongside them, get to know them, and *serve them* with our time. I can think of little else more fulfilling than a young person bearing testimony to how the Lord used an older believer to awaken their faith and point them to the gospel. Perhaps a believing teen, who comes to know Jesus or deepens their relationship with Him, will cite you as part of their believer's testimony.

The two most common reasons for lay people not serving in the youth ministry include intimidation and having kids in the youth group. And I get these excuses because I've used them. But they are not hard and fast reasons to turn away from serving teens in this capacity. As far as intimidation goes, many fear they won't be able to answer hard questions, or they fear they won't connect with young people because they're too old. I remember a youth leader in my church growing up who was in her sixties when she accompanied us on a mission's trip. I distinctly recall how much I valued her presence, and while she was the nurse present, she became so much more to the girls on that trip. We bonded with her in a unique way as she was a steady source of comfort and reassurance when it was needed. You're never too old to serve in the youth group; in fact, many teens will appreciate the example of older church members who are willing to give up their time and invest in their life.

Many are also intimidated when it comes to teaching teens. But remember, teenagers aren't looking for someone who has all the "right" answers. The truth as pompous knowledge for the sake of sounding smart will be difficult for a teen to swallow. Their desire is for you to interact with them, listen to them, and just be who you are in Christ. Teens will learn the most from watching how you live out your everyday faith in Jesus. How do you handle conflict as a believer? What do you do when you receive bad news? How do you interact with unbelievers? They need role models – lay people in the church who aren't necessarily paid youth workers – to show them what it looks like to love Jesus in the ordinary means of life. Intimidation comes from feeling like you must put on a show for teens, and they won't respond well to insincere gestures. They will respond to someone who is eager to get to know them, love them, and be transparent with them.

The other common excuse to not serve teens in the youth group is because *you* have teens in the youth group. I get this excuse. I really do, and it's not always best to serve as a regular volunteer in the youth ministry while you have teens involved. But just because you have kids in the youth group does not mean you automatically *shouldn't* serve regularly in the youth group. There are multiple ways to serve the youth ministry without being present on a regular basis, but beyond this, there are some good reasons as to why being a parent of a teen is actually the perfect time to serve in the church's youth group. If you understand you are there to serve the group and not merely parent your child, there can be great benefits both for you and for the teens you're there to serve.

Serving in the group when your own teens are present gives you a unique insight into some of the pressures and struggles that teenagers face. It allows you to be more "in touch" with some of the cultural issues presented from the perspective of varying teens and not just from the viewpoint of your own child. Additionally, serving while you have teens is a great way to get to know your teen's friends in the church, as well as the staff who work with them regularly. You're in the thick of it at home, so you understand more than adults without teens the amount of physical and emotional energy it takes to work with teenagers. Your willingness to serve can be an encouragement to staff and your understanding can be a welcomed gift. Pray earnestly if you feel the Lord leading you to serve teens in this way, seek counsel, and talk with the youth leaders about their needs to see whether your presence in the group gatherings might be helpful.

Serving Teens Beyond Youth Group

If serving in the youth ministry does not seem like the right fit, there are other ways to serve teens in your local church. One of the most significant ways is to simply get to know them. I've had three teenagers, so I know they are not always the easiest to get to know, but, as I've already touched on, that connectedness matters. What can you do this Sunday to get to know one of the teens in your midst just a little better than you do now? When there's a moment for it, ask one of them how their school year is going and what has been good and what has been hard. Be sincere in your questioning and know that, yes, some might look at you like you have a third eye, but you'll also find some who are willing to dialogue, and those willing conversations are the best way to begin getting to know the teens in your church. In getting to know them, you can better serve them, especially if the dialogue eventually turns into a meaningful mentorship. It's vital that teens see the adults that surround them not just as leaders or out-of-touch adults who don't really care about what they're going through, but that they see adults as potential friends who are willing and wanting to invest in them and get to know them. I think teens are often underestimated. We have so much to learn from what they face daily, how they interact with unbelievers in our current day, and from the ways they view the world. If it seems impossible that you might learn from a teen or vice versa, God can do it! Don't expect less than big things when you pray for the Lord to reveal how you might serve the teens in your church.

But we also serve the teens in our church by simply involving them in the life of the church. Don't make sweeping generalizations about teenagers and view them as a group only able to help with menial jobs. Many of them are pursuing Jesus in big ways, and they are ready to serve using their giftedness. For the sake of the body, we should be readily looking for ways we can include their gifts and talents in the life of the church. Are the teens involved in corporate worship in your church? There are often teens with incredible music expertise and other gifts that can be a huge blessing to a congregation. In our Scripture reader rotation, we have high school students sign up from time to time, and one week a teen signed up who had not read before. When she began, I was taken aback by how beautifully she communicated the passage. Her diction, her tone, and her sincerity made the Scripture come alive. I later told her she had a true gift for reading Scripture, and I believe God will continue to use this gift in His kingdom.

Student leaders, if youth groups have this sort of thing, can benefit by learning from the leaders of the church, and involving them in some of the ins and outs of church life is a way of contributing to the next generation of leaders in the church. It also serves our teens as a way of showing them that they are as important as any adult who desires to learn and serve. We must communicate to our teens the truth that they are necessary to the body, and that we need them and their giftedness. Jesus not only welcomes the littlest child, but He loves our teenagers more than we will ever be able to understand. May our churches emulate that love by serving the teens in our midst.

32

Cultivating a Desire to Serve God's People in Young Children

My daughter traveled to Africa for a mission's trip when she was in high school. While the trip itself was just over a week, the whole of the experience lasted several months. There were fundraising letters written and sent out, team meetings that took place, daily prayer times over the people they would encounter, and vaccines that needed to be scheduled. It was a lot of work, but for her to have the most fruitful experience when we sent her off with the team, we needed to put the time into walking alongside our daughter through the preparation necessary for this important and formative trip.

In the same way, teaching children to serve by using their gifts to show love for God and love for others is an essential part of the preparation for the day when your child will leave the nest and create their own faith liturgies. We have the privilege of walking alongside them through this important preparation. As we've already established, teaching children to serve does not ensure they will remain in the church. Their heart toward God and His church is ultimately the Lord's work, but there is no doubt that testimony after testimony bears witness to the connectivity that a child had in the church later impacting their involvement in it as an adult.

Parents may fear that encouraging their child to do some kind of work in the church will cause them to turn away from it, so many prefer to keep church related activities to ones where their son or daughter can simply enjoy themselves and have fun while still learning about Jesus. The problem with this mindset is that we're introducing a consumeristic view of the church at an early age when we teach our kids that church is just about them being served, and this is a *very difficult mindset to change* the older a child becomes. Though it might seem counterintuitive, the places children serve are often the places they have the most fun. As it is with adults, when children serve together, they build unique relationships within the church body, many times across generations, and they better understand what it means that their Savior came to earth not to be served but to serve. This understanding naturally bleeds over into every aspect of a child's life whether it's their view of chores or their relationships with siblings and friends. As their little hearts begin to better grasp that their hands and feet were not just made for receiving, they will more likely be willing to readily offer their service into adulthood.

And don't underestimate the powerful ways God can use the service of children. I think of 1 Samuel 16 where David, a young shepherd boy, served in the presence of a tormented king. God used David's musical ability, even at a young age, to bring refreshment and reprieve to King Saul. And in John 6, we read about a boy who God used to help feed thousands of people with his five barley loaves and two fish. God could have chosen an adult's food with which to perform this miracle, but John points out in his Gospel that it is a boy the Lord approaches. This young child is not overlooked by Jesus in the crowd, but Jesus sees the boy, and He uses what the child has to show His majesty and His glory to all who are present. God can and will use the young in His church in big and miraculous ways. Their service is no less important than any teen or adult in the church. Because this is true, it's so important that we're cultivating in our children a desire to be used by God in their service to others.

Teach why we serve

The reason *why* we do this is an essential part of the cultivation. It's easy for children to become confused about the reasoning if our service is reduced to a religious duty that we check off our weekly to-do list. Instead, by the grace of God, teach children that we serve others in the church and in our communities *because we have a relationship with Jesus.* Explaining service cannot and should not be done without explaining both the necessity of loving and serving God and showing His love to others. Serving others without a proper understanding of why we serve can become a legalistic duty or a mere humanitarian effort. On the other extreme, teaching only the importance of loving God misses Scripture's clear exhortation that part of the way we show our love and dedication to the Lord is *through* our service to others (Gal. 5:13-14). This is why it's vital to have children join you in your service both inside and outside the church. They need to see what the activity of service looks like outside of simply praying for people who are in need. This understanding starts with you, mom and dad. Your kids watch the ways you use your giftedness in the church whether you realize it or not, and they are learning from what they observe. Why are you serving? Start there. Do you serve grudgingly or, in the strength of Christ, do you offer yourself to God's people with joy because you love Jesus with all your heart? Pray for grace each morning, that the Lord might give you exactly what you need to serve with a willing heart and with the joy of the Lord. Your children will learn from you as you learn from your Father what it means to serve Him and serve His people.

Equally important when teaching children about serving is to include a conversation about work in God's house. One day a child will be old enough to work for pay, but even then, it's important that they understand that their work can, and should, provide something that is for the good and the service of their neighbor. But before they work for pay, and as they work for pay, they should always leave room to serve in their church. Embracing the importance of this begins in our homes when we teach our children what is expected around the house, not for money but because they are members of the household. Whether it's taking clothes out of the dryer or putting dishes in the dishwasher, there are activities they can do as members of your family contributing to the betterment of the family unit. In the same way, we teach our children that God's household does not function properly without their serving hands. Their extended family needs their little hands and feet to serve for the betterment of the family unit.

Practical Ways to Cultivate Service in Children

There are a myriad of ways to involve our children in serving God's people. Most of these can be done with you or another adult, which is one of the greatest ways for a child to feel connected into the church community, but many can be done by themselves or with a Sunday School group. Here are just a few of the examples of ways children can serve their church body:

1. When there is an individual or a team traveling for a mission's trip, have them draw a picture of the participants and pray for them each night while they are away.
2. Print out pictures of the missionaries your church supports and tell your child about the area in which that person is serving. Discuss the potential challenges to spreading the gospel in their part of the world. Have your child then write a letter to the missionary and family.
3. Sharpen and restock pencils both in the church pews and in the classrooms.
4. Clear the bulletins from the pews or chairs after worship.

5. Have your child assist you in making snacks for Sunday fellowship.
6. Help collect the offering.
7. Help greet people at the door and pass out bulletins when congregants come in for worship.
8. Sing in the church's children's choir. This is often overlooked as an act of service, but this is different from singing in a school or community choir in that most church choirs participate in worship from time to time. In this way, we are teaching our children what it looks like to serve the body by leading the congregation in worship.
9. Talk to your children about what they are good at. This can be a very fun discussion with young children as they are often not shy about sharing their giftedness. Once you've made a list, help them to think through ways they can use their gifts to serve others in the church.
10. Bring your child along, if possible, to an area of service where God has called you outside of the church. This is so formative for our young children.

I remember visiting a refugee family one thanksgiving when my kids were very young. We brought the family dinner and visited for a few hours. Not only did my kids have an unexpectedly joy-filled thanksgiving, but they still remember that holiday of service. Friendships were made, lessons of thanksgiving were learned, and both families were filled with gratitude.

There are so many other ideas that could be added to this list, but what's important is that the reason for service is clear and that service is happening in some capacity. Encourage them in these young and formative years by explaining just how important they are to the body of Christ. Show them, with even their little acts of service, how valuable their gifts are to the ministry and life of the church.

33

Cultivating a Desire to Serve God's People in Teens

There are a few teens in our church whom I have watched in awe over the past few years because of their willingness to serve selflessly. One sweet young man brings his younger sibling to the midweek children's ministry activities and stays to help put away the tables and chairs. Another young man serves in our AV ministry throughout the year and has even shown up at 5:30 am to help with sound for an Easter sunrise service. And one young woman serves in the nursery for our midweek children's ministry. Each Wednesday we meet, she is there, excited and ready to love on the kids in our church. None of these teens is paid for these jobs, but they all do it willingly, and I'm consistently humbled by their service. In my gratitude, I find myself wondering: why do they do this for our church? Do their parents slip them a twenty and tell them to go do something good?

I can assure you that is not the case as most do these acts of service without even being asked, but I have honestly wondered what motivates these teens to serve the body of Christ. As I reflected on this question, I thought about two things that all three of these teens have in common. The first is that their parents all serve regularly in the church. The second is that these three teens have connected into church outside of merely showing up for worship on a Sunday morning.

I don't think what these teens have in common is insignificant in their eagerness to serve in God's house. Parents who set the example and teens who feel like they belong to their church are the starting places in cultivating a heart of service in the hearts of our teenagers. If you are not giving your time inside and outside of the church, that's the place to start, parent. And if you are, the next step is praying about how to help your teen connect into their local church. To do this, they need to feel like they have a sense of purpose and belonging in the church. And sometimes serving provides that intergenerational connectedness which becomes the answer to their purpose and belonging.

Sadly, many teens in the church don't feel like they are a necessary part of the body of Christ and perceive their service to be unneeded or they perceive service in general as something merely "for the adults." It's so important that we teach our teens that when Paul talks about the necessity of the various body parts within a church in 1 Corinthians 12, he is referring to *all in the church*, the young people included. Imagine if the only ones serving had sixty-year-old eyes or seventy-year-old legs. It sure wouldn't work well. We need the strength, creativity, and energy of the teens in our churches. They are a necessary part of the body, and this needs to be reinforced over and over. Serving others can be the spark that ignites a stagnant faith. I had this experience as a teenager, and I've heard many young adults who bear witness to God using their service to deepen their relationship with Jesus.

Will you always encounter a willing and eager attitude when you suggest serving to your teen? *Absolutely not.* Even as adults, we sometimes answer needs begrudgingly. If service is something your teen is unfamiliar with or if they have done it infrequently, then you will be especially likely to experience resistance. I remember one summer telling one of my teens that they needed to find a place to serve one time a week. I was hopeful with his quiet contemplation as I imagined him mulling over the many possible places he could serve. Instead, after a brief time of reflection, my teen looked at me and said matter-of-factly: *"No thanks. I think I'd rather just chill this summer."*

Most, though not all, may not be naturally inclined to be proactive in finding places to serve whether it's inside or outside the church. However, as is the case with most things while our children are living under our roof, it's OK to require serving in some capacity. There are many aspects of our teens' daily life that we consider non-negotiables. I'm sure you can name at least three things right now that you require of your teen, whether it's school, chores, or being consistent in a commitment to an extracurricular activity. But when it comes to participating in the life of the church and serving God's people, parents are often very reticent to "require" it of their teen. There's no doubt this is a nuanced issue, as we've already touched on, but like anything that we make a "norm," that life liturgy will often carry into adulthood.

When my son was about eight, I put him in a suit for Easter Sunday morning that he *hated*. It was a three-piece suit that he deemed "the most uncomfortable thing that had ever touched his body," and he complained the entire morning. One of our staff members who observed (and heard) the ongoing complaints from my son tried to turn his complaint into a game: "Jrod, if you wear that suit every day for one year, I'll give you a prize." Not knowing what the prize would be, my competitive son could not turn down the challenge, so it was agreed upon with a handshake. For one entire year, my son wore that suit *every single Sunday*. Toward the end of the twelve months, the sleeves were too short, the pants looked like a flood was expected, and random church members left bags of boy's clothes in my husband's office concerned for the boy who, apparently, had only one Sunday outfit.

But here's what's interesting. He complained about the suit for the first several weeks, but eventually wearing it just became a part of his routine. In fact, wearing it was so ingrained that the week after the one-year mark, my son almost put the suit back on. It was mom who said enough was enough. But kids are like this! What is new or uncomfortable will be met with resistance, but the more they do it, the less they complain because it just becomes a natural part of their daily life.

As we've talked about in earlier chapters, the older a teen gets, the laxer our reins should be in what we require in their commitment to the church because talking through their decisions to get involved or not while they're still in our house can have lifelong benefits. But it's reasonable to expect some form of service in the years our kids are adolescents. And one of the best places for your teen to start serving is in their local church. When they are regularly contributing to the life of the church, it can solidify their feeling of belonging and connectedness.

Beyond feeling like they have purpose in their church, when teens serve God's people, there is an opportunity for personal growth and character building. There is not a better way to learn selflessness and compassion than serving those who are younger and older, and it's also a wonderful way for a teen to better understand their giftedness. Serving in our youth's worship team is where I discovered for the first time a passion for leading worship, and I know many discover for the first time that they have a gift they didn't know about until they used it to serve in God's house. Whether it's reading Scripture, serving on the worship team, ushering on a Sunday morning, or helping with Vacation Bible School, these can be incredible opportunities for our teens to grow spiritually and emotionally as they discover the unique ways God has gifted them.

As is the case when our teens are younger, we don't want them to view their service as a mere religious obligation, but the prayer is that they understand that part of the way they express their love for Jesus is by loving and serving His bride.

It may not always happen easily or naturally, but the more they do it, the more they are fostering a sense of purpose and nurturing a lifelong commitment to faith and service. We need the teens of our church, brothers and sisters, and we need to communicate this regularly because their involvement and giftedness will assuredly contribute to the overall health and vitality of our churches.

Conclusion

Every few years, Christmas falls on a Sunday. When this happened a few years ago, the arguments over having church or not on Christmas Sunday morning were pervasive. There were tweets defending why churches *must* keep their doors open Christmas Sunday, and then other posts which argued that the sabbath begins at sundown Saturday; therefore, Sunday church was not necessary after a Christmas Eve service. The floodgates of comments and opinions were unleashed, and they engulfed social media.

Some of the uglier comments on the differing sides were not surprising, unfortunately, but what I found almost unbelievable was that the subject took center stage amongst church leaders and their parishioners. I struggled with the arguing, but mostly, I was confused. To be in God's house worshipping with His people is a privilege, and it's one I fear that many Christians in the Western word have become apathetic about. Christians in other parts of the world would quite literally give their life to be in God's house on Christmas morning.

For some, church has become a mere chore that is "done" reluctantly. Perhaps it's a dispirited duty, leaving many longing for reasons to take extended breaks from its community. Resentment rises when this is the prominent attitude, and the church is easily reduced to a group of lost sheep who are unaware and out of touch. If that's the case, it's no wonder that for some an opportunity to cancel was harshly defended and argued.

For others, church has been reduced to duty that is checked off simply to feel better about oneself. In this legalistic frame of mind, it's no wonder that the attitude toward those who cancelled was a prideful, *"shame on you."* Church for these can too easily become a self-righteous badge of honor that can become more important than Jesus.

We all have the tendency to err on one side or the other, but neither attitude is how God intended for us to perceive His bride. At its essence, the body of believers in a local church is held together and maintained by Jesus' love for us and by our love for one another as spiritual brothers and sisters (Eph. 4:15-16). And sometimes it's a messy love, as illustrated through the prophet Hosea.

God commands this prophet to take a prostitute for his wife and, although she continues to betray his commitment, Hosea stays with her, loves her, and is faithful to her. Hosea's story of unrelenting love is a picture of what it is like for Christ to love His church. Jesus loves relentlessly, and He delights in His children wholly and completely, even when they act unfaithfully. This persistent, never-ending love is what the church is built on. When we begin to understand the magnificence of it, there is little more profound than returning praise to Jesus *in His house* and *with His people*. It is a privilege that we do not deserve. And God's amazing love is tangibly experienced through the church community that we stand shoulder to shoulder with, and it's most deeply felt when we press in by serving, worshipping, gathering, sharing, and fellowshipping together.

Apathy is crushed when we feel that love through a hug, or through a saint willing to sit for a few extra minutes to pray on behalf of a situation that feels overwhelming. The begrudging attitude softens when we discover the beauty in heartfelt worship because of answered prayers, in sincere singing through tears because God has not left us alone in our battles, and through the preaching of the Word as God speaks directly to us, penetrating our prideful heart. This community, the bride of Christ, He gives as a gift for us to feel, see, experience, and better understand the love that Jesus has for His people.

The year of the bickering over Christmas Sunday services, my husband and I arrived early on Christmas Eve to prepare for our annual candlelight service. When we arrived, we were met with a flooded building due to a burst pipe. Panic rushed through as we watched the surge of water pour out the back doors of the church. I walked through the halls, my shoes entirely under cold water, and held back tears as we made calls cancelling all services for the Christmas weekend. I couldn't help but think about the online bantering. Perhaps it's when we *can't* meet, that our arguing over whether to or not becomes nonsensical.

The first parishioner who arrived assessed the flooded building and then said to me with tenderness, "*Let's get to work.*" Within an hour, the flood was overcome by church members who arrived not in their beautiful Christmas garb, but in their work boots and with their cleaning equipment, ready to serve and love the body of Christ. I will always remember that Christmas Eve gathering, as unorthodox and messy as it was, as one of the most beautiful pictures of the church I have ever seen.

When was the last time you took a step back to appreciate the beauty of the church even in all its messiness? I mean, when was the last time you really stopped to look around and take in the gift that is Christ's bride? Whether it's from the back row or the front, *look around, believer.* The church is God's gift for you. We don't commit to it because of perfect leaders, we don't serve it because of some high pay, and we don't love its people because there is no mess involved. *We love and serve the church because we love and serve Jesus.* Just as a bride is cherished by her groom with all her imperfections, so Jesus deeply loves and values His church. Through the ongoing ministries and relational touchpoints, the church lives out its identity as that beloved bride until the day when we will all rejoice together at the marriage feast of the Lamb.

And until that day comes, *let's get to work.* Let's get beyond being a spectator or skeptic from the back row and get busy asking God to refocus our vision. Pray boldly that we might see the church in the way God sees her, that we might embrace her in the way God loves her, that we might serve her in the way Jesus taught us to serve, and that we might pass on to the next generation the beauty of God's church.

Also available from Christian Focus Publications...

Why we need the Church
(and why the Church needs us)

WHO NEEDS THE
CHURCH?

TERRY JOHNSON

978-1-5271-0835-6

Who Needs the Church?
Why We Need the Church (and Why the Church Needs Us)

Terry L. Johnson

A thought-provoking introduction to the importance of the local church

It seems that increasing numbers of professing Christians in the West do not attend church. Church, to many, has become a place to go when it is convenient, to have one's needs met. Terry L. Johnson asks whether our individualistic, dismissive attitude to the gathering of the local church can be squared with that of the New Testament.

Examining what the Bible has to say about the church, Johnson shows why the local body of believers is an essential part of the life of every believer – and the role that each individual believer plays in the life of the church. This thought-provoking, challenging book will benefit every believer.

Christian Focus Publications

Our mission statement
Staying Faithful

In dependence upon God we seek to impact the world through literature faithful to His infallible Word, the Bible. Our aim is to ensure that the Lord Jesus Christ is presented as the only hope to obtain forgiveness of sin, live a useful life and look forward to heaven with Him.

Our Books are published in four imprints:

◁○✕ CHRISTIAN FOCUS

Popular works including biographies, commentaries, basic doctrine and Christian living.

◁○✕ MENTOR

Books written at a level suitable for Bible College and seminary students, pastors, and other serious readers. The imprint includes commentaries, doctrinal studies, examination of current issues and church history.

◁○✕ CHRISTIAN HERITAGE

Books representing some of the best material from the rich heritage of the church.

◁○✕ CF4KIDS

Children's books for quality Bible teaching and for all age groups: Sunday school curriculum, puzzle and activity books; personal and family devotional titles, biographies and inspirational stories – because you are never too young to know Jesus!

Christian Focus Publications Ltd,
Geanies House, Fearn, Ross-shire,
IV20 1TW, Scotland, United Kingdom.
www.christianfocus.com